To Karen —

your support of
Origin - Napa helps
Preserve Napa
Valley - Tom Cahill

AT FAMILY HOME 6/4/04
TO OUR PAST & FUTURE!

THE MIND AGE SERIES

A BOOK FROM
THE MIND AGE SERIES

NAPA VALLEY

Edited by Patton Howell

with

Mary Ann McComber and Ruth Berggren

Donald McComber, Lawrence Barker, Joan Howell

Saybrook Publishing Co., Inc.

San Francisco   Dallas

First Saybrook trade paperback edition published 2000

Library of Congress Cataloging-in-Publication Data
00 133459
CIP

edited by Howell, Patton with McComber, Mary Ann and Berggren, Ruth; McComber, Donald; Barker, Lawrence; Howell, Joan

Napa Valley, edited by Patton Howell, Mary Ann McComber and Ruth Berggren, Donald McComber, Lawrence Barker, Joan Howell
p. cm.

ISBN 0-933071-34-5 (pbk.)

1. Napa Valley – anthology by residents. 2. USA – a new vision of community. 3. Howell, Patton et al. 4. Travel Essays

Saybrook Publishing Company, Inc.
5307 McCommas
Dallas, Texas 75206

Printed in the United States of America

This book is dedicated to the
"collective individuals" of
Napa Valley.

The profits from the sales
go to the
Queen of the Valley Hospital Foundation
for a healthy community in
Napa Valley.

This is a book of voices, people speaking about their community. Not only is there a rhythm within these voices, there is a rhythm between voices. Cathy Lombardi is an old friend of Saybrook Publishing Co. and has preserved these rhythms in her art of typesetting. Marcelline Watson, our production manager, has worked with us for forty years. She has made this book possible. Another old friend, Fred Huffman, created our cover showing Mount St. Helena covered with snow. This usually happens in January and brings everyone out to enjoy it. The landscape is still green. The artistic impression of the building shown is the Christian Brothers Winery. Readers have been Dr. Rick Lange, for whom the book was a reminder of the conversation of old friends sitting around a fire. Randy D. Gordon L.L.P. located the rhythms of highs and lows for us. Thank you all.

CONTENTS

ACKNOWLEDGMENTS

We acknowledge the help and support of the thousands of people who, just by living in Napa Valley, created together a new vision of community. In addition are the loving, generous friends who have personally helped and supported the three-year development of the book.

Aimee Price
Babe Learned
Bill and Lila Jaeger
Brian Kelly
Carolyn Saunders
Dan Duckhorn
Don McComber
Father Brenkle
Hugh Davies
Martha May
Jean Michels
Jim Gamble
Nancy Garden
Jaime Aguirre
John Salmon
Margrit Biever Mondavi
Lorraine Kongsgaard
Robin Rose
Justin Meyer
Liz Martini
Toby Wolf
Mel Varrelman
Hilary Stanton Zunin
Ren Harris
Mark Luce
Bob Trinchero
Mike Rippey
Jeff Redding
Kathryn Winter
John Dunlap
Pat and Bob Gustafson
Helen Megan
David Berggren
Richard Larson
Ralph and Melinda Mendelson
Jim McIntosh
Don and Pati Simon
Don and Kathi Turner
Denise Schubert
Norm Kraus
Carol Lyon
Judith Branzburg
Alice Petty

Andrew Hoxsey
Beth Novak Milliken
Brad Wagenknecht
Brother Timothy
Dan Corsello
Dana Leavitt
Dorothy Lind
Giulia Santi
Steve Lundin
Ron Birtcher
Jamie Davies
Tom Gamble
Ramon Viera
William Jarvis
Robert Mondavi
Tom Kongsgaard
Rosemary Partridge
Netty Ensminger
Robin Lail
Rich Salvestrin
Charlie Toledo
Sandra Learned Perry
Leonard Zunin, M.D.
Guy Kay
Tony Holzhauer
Mark Aubert
Anna True
Hugo Rossi
Elaine Hudson
Leona and Gordon Biddle
Elvon Harris
Stephen Berggren
Ken Berggren
Paul Larson
Sally Seymour
Dale and Annie Schwarzhoff
Ron and Carolyn Tapper
Carole and Richard Williams
Randy Miller
Diane Price
Lonne Carr
Amy Ryan

INTRODUCTION
by
Patton Howell

All over the world people speak of Napa Valley, but they are not only thinking of Napa wine and food. They are thinking of a place with a unique way of living. Some say it is a vision for a new kind of community. Napa is a community all its own; a place where a person might live a whole life and consider it complete. It is an intellectual place. A place of art and theater and some of the best cooking in the world. An open-handed American generosity for both the poor and the rich have blended together with the ancient art of growing grapes for wine. It is a new place for business and government where the people themselves decide directly what they need rather than what business or government decides.

The extinct volcano of Mount St. Helena stands at and closes the northern end of the valley. Look down on Napa Valley from its summit, you see a great unfenced park. From the top of this ancient volcano, looking south, you see fields of vines. Forests sweep up to the sheltering embrace of two mountain ranges on either side of the valley. Evergreens blanket the Mayacama Mountains on the west and stately oak trees dot the hillsides on the east. The Napa River starts at the foot of Mt. St. Helena and empties into San Francisco Bay on the south. Follow the river down, until it makes a great oxbow in the town of Napa, nearly coming back on itself.

Share the stories of the people who have built the valley, and the people whose ways of living are nurtured in their towns and vine-yards and forests. These voices belong to people embarked on a new vision of community. They speak to anyone in any community. In extraordinary times, people sometimes do extraordinary things without realizing it.

Stand here on this mountaintop, you can see the valley as a whole. Stretch out your arm to the valley. You see from this vantage point that it will all fit in the palm of your hand. Hold this valley in your hand and possess the intimate thoughts of the valley people who created it. Hold it in your hand; it will travel with you wherever you go.

I
The
River

How The American Center for Wine, Food, and the Arts Came to Napa

by Dorothy Lind

The American Center for Wine, Food, and the Arts is set on 3.5 acres in downtown Napa on the oxbow of the Napa River. Dorothy Lind is the CEO of the Napa Valley Exposition.

The Napa Valley has ancient untouched energy. It's very powerful. It's powerful in the way that it's beautiful. It's powerful in the way you can put anything in the ground and it grows. It is so strong that the people who are drawn here understand it. You look at the people who come to the Napa Valley—the Bob Mondavis of the world. Bob Mondavi went around saying, "I'm going to start my own winery by borrowing money from a beer company, and I'm going to make my wines great. I'm going to make sure that everybody else's wines are great, and we're going to have the best wines in the world. We're going to compete against the European market and we're going to win." People said, "You're nuts!" Here's this same guy at 85 saying, "I did what I knew I needed to do. I gave the gift. I believed in it. What I got was so powerful. What I understood was that the world was nothing but unconditional love. I need to give that back. I need to understand that many of the things that I created in making California wines wonderful, in making the Napa Valley incredible, also created traffic and lots of other issues. I want to make sure that I continue to resolve those issues, that I go on creatively looking at the bigger picture and coming up with solutions."

Robert Mondavi talked about doing his Center for Wine, Food, and the Arts originally next to the winery, then on a hill in Oakville, then maybe in Yountville, and possibly in St. Helena. I said to a few of my friends, "The city of Napa needs magic. It needs someone to believe in it. It needs to take its rightful place in the valley. The American Center should be here." I tried to talk to him at the time. We weren't that close, but we knew each other. He considered me "the little pest from the fairgrounds who keeps bothering me." I said, "If you are truly a visionary, you should help create an urban river restoration project. Anybody can build on a hill in Yountville. Anybody can build on a hill in Oakville. Anybody can build on a hill in St. Helena. But it takes a real visionary to understand that if the city of Napa doesn't work, the whole valley won't work. It needs to come into its own. We need to restore this river." Other people around Bob said, "She's nuts!"

Moira Johnston Block and I had formed a group called The Friends of the River to raise consciousness about the Napa River and its potential. We needed to educate people about the river, how important the history is, what the city of Napa has, its history. Since I run a fairgrounds, the best way I could think of doing this was to put on a play. Moira and her husband had party boats—pontoon boats where you can get six people on a boat—and their neighbors had pontoon boats. We had three pontoon boats! This was like the Pinta, Nina, and Santa Maria going down the Napa River! I said, "Let's do a pontoon boat trip. Let's invite Bob and Margrit, and the guys from UC Davis, and David Wolper and Phil Williams of Phil Williams and Associates, the great river restoration environmentalists who have a wonderful engineering firm in San Francisco. Let's stage a great drama on the Napa River. We'll go to the library and research the history of Napa, and we'll write a script." My husband and her husband told us we were nuts. Randy Starbuck, the redevelopment director at the time, took the third pontoon boat. We wrote a script about the history of the Napa River, starting with the Wappo Native Americans, then going to the General Vallejo midcentury era, and then to Nathan Coombs who founded the city.

On the day of the boat trip, I wear a dress that I bought at the mercado in San Antonio—this big black dress with gigantic fish on it—and big earrings. Moira has the same dress. Margrit Mondavi has the same earrings. My goal was to see if there was some way I could make a trade for free or cheap land from the state. The land we were thinking of using at that time for the American Center was the fairgrounds—35 acres—and part of the Vallergas property—another

13 acres across the river from us. So I called the Governor's office and asked if they would send somebody down to go on this boat trip. I wanted very prestigious people. Senator Mike Thompson was there. Senator Ken Maddy was there. It was a high-powered group of folks spread out on these three party boats.

The Governor's office sends a guy named John Salmon. This guy was the Governor's representative for all state property. I'd never met him before. He was told, "Go down to Napa. Meet the fair manager on the Fourth Street dock on a Friday." He's thinking, "Why am I doing this? I don't want to meet this fair manager." But he shows up. All the rest of us are dressed in very festive boating clothes— casual, because that's Napa. If you dress up, you have no money. If you look really awful, with dirty jeans and boots, you've got a lot. Everybody in Napa knows that. This poor guy shows up in a three-piece power suit. He has his white shirt and his power Republican red tie and his little gold cufflinks.

I say, "Hi! It's me!" And he looks at me like, "Who is this woman in this weird dress and huge earrings?" I'm introducing him to all these people, and he's watching the champagne being loaded onto the boats, and all the beautiful food. Now he's thinking, "I can do this."

We sit down in the boats. Bob Mondavi, Joe Vallerga, and John Salmon (the guy with the land deals) are with me. Right away, I ask John, "Hey, can you make us a deal for a bunch of state land for nothing?" The guy says, "Sure." And I say, "Deal!" I turn to Bob and say, "See, Bob, we can make this work!" And Bob says, "OK!" We start down the river, and the guy from the Governor's office is thinking, "Am I part of the cast? This is some kind of a ruse . . . and I'm not sure who the target is here, but I'm afraid it might be me."

We go about 10 minutes down the river. Moira and Randy Starbuck are on the other boats, reading from the same script. "Let me tell you about the history of the Napa River. It's one of only three navigable rivers in the state of California. You can go from the city of Napa to Tokyo if you want to." We talk about the history of the river. We get into the Wappo culture and what their history was like. We come around the first river bend, and there's an Indian on the riverbank, with long black hair, and he's holding a big salmon, and he says in Wappo, "Welcome back to the river." He yells it out. And then he yells in English, "Welcome back to the river." Bob Mondavi says, "My god, I had no idea we had salmon that size in the Napa River." Joe Vallerga, who owns the local grocery store, says, "Give me a break. Dorothy made me get that out of the deli counter at six this morning." John Salmon asks, "Who's the Indian?" I say, "That's my forklift driver." He's 19 years old. He's dressed in a loincloth and a Tina Turner wig. This poor kid is totally embarrassed in my office that morning, putting this loincloth on and the Tina Turner wig. But from the bank he looks pretty good. "Welcome back to the river!"

John Salmon is rolling his eyes, thinking, "Oh, my god! I sure hope the food is good!" Joe Vallerga is laughing. Bob and Margrit are having a wonderful time. We're pouring the champagne. We're going down the river. Half an hour later, we get to the next bend, and there's mariachi music. On the bank, there is a young man and his wife, holding a baby. He yells out, "Welcome back to the river! I'm General Vallejo. This is my wife and my son. We're so glad to see you!" That's my maintenance man, his wife, and their three-month-old baby, and a mariachi band from Yountville. They're playing away, and they're throwing roses out to the river. It's wonderful. Bob is saying, "This is incredible! This is so wonderful!"

I've got my radio with me, and I start to hear grumblings: "Dorothy! Dorothy!" Normally the weather is not that hot in May, but this day was about 85 degrees, and I know it's Joe Anderson (the assistant manager of the fairgrounds) who is dressed in buckskin and fur, along with Pam Walker, portraying his wife (who is the Executive Director of the downtown merchants). They are Mr. and Mrs. Nathan Coombs, the founders of the city of Napa. Joe's saying, "I'm hot as hell! Where are you? You're an hour late!" We're drinking, and laughing and talking, and going through the history of Napa. We're having a wonderful time, and poor Joe's getting really hot. I say, "We're coming! We'll be there in about fifteen minutes." We come around to the city of Napa and China Peak, which is where the city was founded, and there are Joe and Pam as Mr. and Mrs. Nathan Coombs, dressed up in buckskin and fur and a long dress. Pam has a dozen red roses. She walks out into the river, gets wet, and hands Margrit and Bob a dozen roses. They introduce themselves as Mr. and Mrs. Nathan Coombs, the founders of Napa, and they say, "Welcome back to the river. This is your home. This is the river that winds through the entire Napa Valley. This is our heart. Welcome back to the river."

Bob Mondavi stands up in the boat and says, "I will build the Center for Wine, Food, and the Arts in the city of Napa. I will help restore this river." And that was the beginning.

> *The American Center for Wine, Food, and the Arts is a cultural center whose mission is "to explore, integrate, and celebrate wine and food in relation to the other arts in expressing and creating our unique American sensibility." Its 80,000-square-foot main pavilion is scheduled to open in the Fall of 2001. In conjunction with the renovation of the Margrit Biever Mondavi Opera House Theatre on Main Street (a vintage 1880 opera house which will reopen in 2002 with a 450-seat theatre), the Oxbow School for the Arts on Third Street (a semester-long boarding school integrating arts into the curriculum), the development of the Napa Exposition Center across Third Street, and other private redevelopment enterprises, The American Center signals a renaissance in the town of Napa.*

How a Community Came to Terms
with its River

by David G. Dickson

The Napa River is a thread through the Napa Valley, and it
levels out and meets up with the San Francisco Bay Estuary in the
major urban center of the Napa Valley, the city of Napa. It is not so
remarkable that the city sits where it does. The city, centered where
the river meets Napa Creek and the oxbow, a great big turn in the
river, is the furthestmost navigable point on the Napa River Estuary.
The tides come in and out up to this point, about a third of the way
up the 55-mile length of the river, from the headwaters on Mt. St.
Helena to the San Pablo Bay.

The Napa Valley community has had a love-hate relationship
with its river since it was settled in the mid-1800s. Napa is the most
flood-prone community in California, even though we have a total
population of only 126,000 people. The Napa River has recorded
27 major floods. In the heart of downtown Napa, the river can carry
only 20,000 cubic feet per second. In 1986, in the largest flood in
Napa's recorded history, close to twice that volume overflowed the
riverbanks.

As with most rivers around the world, each time a flood happens,
the community goes into crisis. It is best described by that knot in
your stomach when you know people are being traumatized in your
community, especially the elderly and more vulnerable, who invariably
end up living in the floodplain because that is the cheapest housing.
One also is thankful for the emergency response system—the fire
departments and human service system, the shelters and the police,
the water rescuers, the volunteers who bring food to the shelters, and

the innkeepers who provide rooms to the evacuees. It is government at its best! It was not that way in the 1986 flood, because there had not been a major flood in about 15 years, and people forget about floods quickly.

In the small town of Yountville, halfway up the Napa Valley, one-third of the town's housing stock is in the mobile home parks, which were built in the 1960s, before floodplain regulations. These folks are the ones that I think about during high water, and I get that knot in my stomach.

Our community has tried to fashion a solution to this major community problem for its entire history. Since the 1960s, not less than four U.S. Army Corps of Engineers (COE) proposals have been presented, voted on, and rejected. The projects proposed in the 1960s, then in the 1970s, and then again in 1995, just did not address the needs of the Napa community, including its migrating fish, its riparian and wetlands, as well as flood protection and flood damage reduction for the 7,000 downtown structures, including its civic center, its people.

Fairly typical and predictable plans for channeling and deepening the river, with extensive flood walls and hard rip-rapped river banks were the standard fare of our Army Corps flood control paradigm. Each plan was better than the last, but they never looked at the problem in terms of the community.

Then a remarkable "coming together" occurred around flood control, which voter surveys said was the Number One issue facing the community. Over a 30-month Community Coalition process, the community's business leaders, environmentalists, government officials, mobile home owners, neighborhoods, fishermen, canoers, Red Cross workers, gadflies, and others participated and coalesced around the concept of a Living River flood protection and restoration plan for the Napa River.

On March 3, 1998, the voters weighed in with the required two-thirds majority to raise taxes in Napa County in order to implement the plan.

I had the once-in-a-lifetime opportunity and privilege to manage the planning process and community-based organizing and compromising structure that had to occur to achieve this community consensus. I was the process architect and manager. I am a self-confessed consensus junky. It comes from my temperament and my dislike of conflict of any kind. I am patient and sometimes suffer from "analysis paralysis."

But I have lived and worked in this community for over 25 years, and I had the network and understanding of the parochial and esoteric political sand traps that exist here.

The first thing our community demanded was that the U.S. Army Corps of Engineers change its relationship with the community. The community wanted to take control of their U.S. Government to make it work for the community. The Corps needed to agree to come out of its offices and mix it up with the community. It needed to hear and listen to us. The San Francisco Bay environmental community had to be embraced and accommodated, because Californians really care about the environment and can be very adamant about it.

Through Senator Barbara Boxer, we got the Corps to the table, agreeing to use the congressional planning appropriation of $1 million to focus on the local Community Coalition process. They needed to "trust the process," but it was a new experience for the Corps in many ways.

The Coalition Steering Committee, composed of local elected officials and the presidents of the Friends of the Napa River, the Napa Valley Economic Development Corporation, and the Wine Institute developed a set of goals. The goals were (1) protection from the 100-year flood; (2) a living, vital Napa River; (3) economic revitalization; (4) a cost that the citizens could support; (5) retaining our valuable federal project authorization (50% funding); and (6) watershedwide planning and a solutions-integrated "system."

In essence, they wanted it all. In order to achieve a two-thirds vote on a tax increase, every influential sector of the community had to be satisfied—in fact excited—about a flood plan. So the goals were then presented to a coalition of 27 local stakeholder organizations to see if they would commit to a process to develop a flood plan addressing all of the goals. If, in the end, they could not, well, at least we had given one last concerted community effort.

Everyone warily agreed to sit at the table and assist in "resourcing" the effort: the Corps as well as the 27 government agencies with jurisdiction over the Napa River and any development within its sphere of influence. Over 24 months, there were eight town-hall-type meetings involving 200–250 of Napa's finest minds who actively participated to conceive a plan, check its constructability and science, and determine its financial feasibility. These meetings became a celebration of progress. Over the first six months, the theme of the Living River became a rallying point, a point of guiding light against which any idea would be tested to determine if it contributed to it or threatened the achievement of that goal.

The hard technical work took place in a continuous process to support the coalition direction. They hammered out financing plans, urban design concepts and standards, and definitions of the Living River based in science. The community learned about things like dissolved oxygen levels, continuous fish and wildlife riparian corridors, geomorphically stable channels, and a river system's natural width-to-depth ratio. We were told how we fit into the big picture by the likes of Luna Leopold, the son of Aldo Leopold, the great environmentalist. Luna is in his late seventies and is considered the father of modern river geomorphology. We had the "battle of the Hydrology Models": the American HEC program versus the Danish Hydraulics Institute's MIKE 11 model.

The old timers here have always believed that no solution was possible because of the tidal action in the Napa River. The scientists sat with the old timers and talked these things out. The scientists had to demonstrate with computer models how the tides interact with the flood flows, and how the Living River Plan accommodated both flows to protect the city from flood damage. We learned right away, of course, that you cannot control floods. You plan for living with them. The lessons of 1993 on the Mississippi River and the Galloway Report were vital to the coalition.

The four technical committees: Living River, Up-Valley watershed management, urban design, and finance & regulatory—each with a cross-section of paid staff, government staff, hired consultants, the Corps of Engineers, and local citizens with special capabilities like landscape architecture, natural resource management, and political organizing—met in the same auditorium each Friday for six months, preparing details to present to the larger Community Coalition.

The community held a celebration of achievement at Chardonnay Hall at the fairgrounds with over 200 coalition participants in June of 1996, when the concept was developed enough to pronounce it a Plan. Then began an eight-to-nine-month period of verification, to see if the details contained a doable plan.

The plan had stiff requirements. We wanted to reconnect the river to its natural floodplain and maintain the natural depth-to-width ratio of the river. In other words, we should widen the river for flood water conveyance, not deepen and channelize it. We wanted to restore historical tidal wetlands and implement watershed management practices to maintain the natural riparian corridors along the river and tributaries. We needed to clean up contaminated river-adjacent properties, replace eight bridges that now act as dams during high flows, and relocate, purchase, or elevate 380 homes and mobile homes that were in the floodplain. There would be required, erosion control plans for all grading, including new vineyards. And we also needed to improve water supply reliability during drought periods, but without increasing water supply for new development.

The plan will cost $250 million. About $100 million will come from the federal government and state environmental restoration grants and highway bridge funding. $150 million will come from local taxpayers and the tourists who visit Napa Valley. A 1/2 percent increase in the local sales tax taps the tourists, who pay about one-third of the local sales tax. This was a very appealing feature of the finance plan to the citizens. Other tax increase proposals were soundly rejected in community surveys conducted under the direction of the Community Coalition.

The tax must expire after 20 years, and two citizen oversight committees were required in the tax measure to scrutinize expenditures and to oversee the technical aspects of project implementation.

Professional public opinion surveys were conducted. By March of 1997, the plan was verified to a point that we knew the voters would support the plan, the COE could participate in an environmentally restorative program of flood management, instead of flood control, and the environmentalists would compromise and ultimately support the tax increase and actively campaign for the effort.

The community coalition process itself became the campaign. All 27 organizations at the table either supported or were silent during the campaign. A well-financed public issue campaign was bankrolled by individual contributions, investments by several large wineries who want to bring the city of Napa into a more intimate relationship with the wine industry and Up-Valley ambience, and by the environmental and business communities. Groups that are usually at odds came together around the flood problems of Napa.

All five cities of the Napa Valley and the county agreed in a Joint Powers written agreement on how the tax proceeds would be equitably shared to address flood protection on a watershedwide basis.

On March 3, 1998, 23,000 Napa County voters turned out in a special election to vote on Measure A, the flood control measure. Only one issue was on the ballot. It was a very high turnout for an election like this. At the end of the evening, the community celebrated victory, with a 300-vote margin. At the end, every participant in the process felt that his or her efforts had made a difference. It was a very sweet victory.

There are many lessons to be learned about community from this success. First, there is a great deal of compassion left in this world. Second, participatory democracy is an excellent model for community decision making. In that process, all ideas must be genuinely heard and considered. People must reach their own conclusions about their pet idea. Because of that, consensus development is a tedious and time-consuming process. Successes like this must be internally motivated.

All government levels were in some way threatened by this planning process. The territorial and conservative nature of bureaucracy is deeply ingrained and hard to change. Populist political pressure is critical to moving these behemoths. Once the decision is made, the bureaucracies and bureaucrats will want to go back to their caves and be left alone to implement the decision. Collaboration is a threat to them.

It is also significant that the scale of the Napa Valley—126,000 in population—is about the size of a single, large neighborhood in an urban center. It is ideal for community decision making. But a planning process like this requires a few totally committed leaders who will live and breathe it for an intense and dedicated period of time. In Napa's case, these individuals included Karen Rippey and Moira Johnston Block, officers of Friends of the Napa River, Steve Kokotas, Executive Director of the Napa Valley Economic Development Corporation, and myself. Others committed extensive time and effort, to be sure. But these leaders were the ones who dedicated their lives for several years, at the expense of other endeavors. No federal or state government mandate can force this kind of process on local communities. It needs to emerge locally, with government agencies supporting and facilitating the process.

The Roundtable

by Ron Birtcher

*John Salmon was asked by the Governor's office: "What
are they doing down in Napa that works? What one thing
would you tell us to do that we can tell other fairgrounds?"
He answered, "Build a big, round table and give it away."*
—Dorothy Lind, CEO of the Napa Valley Exposition

I am past president of the fair board—the Napa Valley Exposition as it is officially called—and was for two years. I've been on the
board for six years. Every foggy night, we get three feet of water in
the fair. We're a logical group to start to try to find a solution to
Napa's flooding problem. Because we are a state agency, we receive
state support. And as a public agency, we are unbiased. We're not
right; we're not left; we're not Up Valley; we're not Down Valley;
we're not east; we're not west. We are just the "fair." We represent
the community. And we're nonprofit. That makes us very credible to
most civic groups and organizations.

Kathleen Heitz Meyers, who was also on the board, suggested
that we have a Roundtable at the fair. If you haven't seen the table,
it's worth looking at, because it's a *big* table. The reason the table is
round is so nobody clamors for the head. Dorothy Lind began to
have meetings with the city, with the county, with the bankers, with
the farmers, with the Up-Valley people, the Middle-Valley people, the
Down-Valley people, the American Canyon people. The table was
designed expressly to get the body politic involved, to get the community involved, to get people together who don't normally sit around
together. We're a free zone in a high war area. We are a treaty table.
We really try, no matter what the issues are, to bring the parties to

16

our table. Whatever is happening in the community, we try to be there and be the balancing home for all the vocalists.

Within communities, you need to have nonprofit, nonpartisan, nonpolitical places where you can bring together lots of people who may have different agendas. If you break up into little special interest groups, community can do nothing. A special interest group may create such noise that government will come along and impose a solution, but that won't be a community solution. That will be government reacting to all the noise being made by these one or two or three or six groups.

When left alone to the squabbling people, government will step in and solve the problem. But I have to tell you, what brings people up quicker than anything—throughout the country, not just here—is the government trying to solve the problem. The very minute that the government agencies, no matter how big or how small the agency is— it could be a little school district, it could be a sanitation district— whenever they rise up above their power level, which most tend to do, then they rise above their capability to function. It's the Peter Principle of government. If you can avoid collapse, you've won the game in government.

I think the purpose of the Roundtable here in Napa is to try to bring all of the forces together, not to overpower the government, but to prevent problems that the government needs to contribute to or try to find solutions for. The way you do that is to bring in, on a regular basis, the old town meeting concept where everybody met in the community church. The idea was: What's going on? What don't you like? And what don't *you* like? And then we'll talk about it and fix it. "We need a horse for the fire engine." So we all go out and solve the problem.

The idea is to solve the problem before it gets out of control, before outsiders solve it or government solves it. Don't let it get to that point. The idea of the Roundtable is the idea of an interactive community—without a purpose being designed. If you say, "We are specifically identifying ourselves as a group that's going to get together to solve issues." That's wrong. What you're there to do is to have a Roundtable to listen to what's going on. The issues will be identified and they'll solve themselves. Because there will be subgroups that will hear the concerns and then there will be a united effort to try to weed through the issues.

So the critical thing is the creation of a forum to let the community come together and let the problems get identified and let solutions get developed that can then be taken to implementation. And to then bring government into it, because these things can't be done without government, but you then have more of a collective approach to it. And it's proactive, because you're identifying the problems before they get to a point where only government can solve it.

It's a People's Forum. Nobody has any motives at the table. When the meeting is called, there is no agenda. From the meeting will come agendas. But the meeting isn't called because the agenda was there first. That really is important. It doesn't always work that way, but that's the intent of the group. There's just stuff out there that needs to be done. Why don't we talk about stuff where your home is. What kind of stuff do you have? Well, I've got potholes. You don't have potholes. That's OK. You're going to have to chip in and pay for our neighbor's potholes. I've got to tell you there's a lot of tears, and there's a lot of pounding and gnashing of teeth, and a lot of other things that happen when I don't always agree with you and you don't always agree with me. But that's what's in this community that's different. How long it's going to last, by the way, I have no idea—but right now it exists in this valley.

If it works for the big picture, does it work in the little picture? Of course, it does. Use that same technique in your own family. Three times a week—or even better, seven times a week—or even one night a week, sit around and just talk a little bit. Look at the issues and say, "What can we do and what needs to change?"

The Miracle of Flood Control

by Dorothy Lind

As we talk about what makes this community unique, and the magic of Napa—it's not the grapes; it's not the vines; it's not the wine; it's not the agriculture; it's the people. It's always the people. There's an enthusiasm in this community—in the whole valley—in finding answers, in not giving up, and in looking at life here as an opportunity. We've got one of the best examples for people learning that they must take responsibility for their future, for their thoughts, for their actions, and for their community in total. It is the Flood Control Project.

We have flooded badly for probably a million years in the Napa Valley. As far back as people can record, about every four or five years, the 100-Year Flood comes and wipes out the Napa Valley. In recent years, the 100-Year Flood comes every two years, and it's devastating. But we keep building. We do dumb things. People do incredibly stupid things—and started doing even dumber things after the 1940s. Before the 1940s, homes in areas that flooded were built up. It doesn't take a lot of brain cells to figure that out: if the flood water is going to go up to here, go about ten feet higher and you won't have to worry about it. Somehow, in the 1950s, we all became brain-dead for about ten years, and people would build homes in the flood plain, low, in the flood's way. And then they'd say, "My god! I got flooded!" In the city of Napa, homes were being built, apartments were being built all over downtown Napa. "What the hell! Let's just build it right there! Sounds good to me!" And we'd flood badly in many of the cities, but in the city of Napa it was particularly ugly, because the river was narrow. It would go around an oxbow, hook, get stuck, and go over everything in its path—mostly the fairgrounds, which is the lowest spot in town. Everybody around us got flooded too. It was devastating. Hundreds of millions of dollars of damage was done in 1986. At the fairgrounds in 1986, we had seven feet of water where the livestock barns are. People were in boats for two days. In 1995, we had 5½ feet of water in the livestock barns. That's how bad it floods in Napa. In 1995, we had two floods. One on January 10th, that was devastating. On March 10th, we had the second one, which was worse. That's when people began to say, "We've got to figure this out."

We have had a Flood Control Project in Napa County on the books of the federal government at the Army Corps of Engineers for decades. In the late 1950s, the Army Corps of Engineers proposed a plan: "Dredge that sucker! Knock it out! If it's going to the right, we'll make it go to the left! We'll put up steel girders and a big wall of cement, and it will look really ugly, but it'll stop that water!" Well, we know how well that worked on the Mississippi River . . . but at that time, that was the thinking: "Just stop it! Man can do anything!"

At that time, if you got 50 percent of the vote, swell, it happened. The folks promoting the first flood control plan had mostly federal money to fix the flooding in Napa, and in the city of Napa only. The public share was a million dollars. But people said, "That's ridiculous! A million dollars!" So they voted it down.

People weren't particularly upset that it was an ugly plan. Nobody wanted to spend the money. They'd say, "How come I have to put any money into this?" After serious flooding again, in the early 1970s, the Board of Supervisors and the City Council in Napa got together and said, "We need another flood control plan." This one was bigger, far more expensive, and even uglier. It was the same kind of thing. "Stick that wall in there. Put up that rebar and steel, and it's going to stop that sucker." And it didn't pass. So, there were two strikes against us.

Then, the Jarvis–Gann initiative was voted in, which means that you have to have a two-thirds majority on any taxing initiative in California to pass it. Seventy percent of the political campaigns for the two-thirds vote fail. As I said, we flooded badly in 1995. In 1995, the flood control plan with the Army Corps of Engineers was still on the books with 50 percent federal funding, so flood control became a huge issue again. A group of leaders, in the early 90s, went back to Washington and asked, "Can we still keep this flood control plan alive?" And the people at the Army Corps of Engineers in Washington looked at their books and said, "Yeah, but we've been dealing with you for 35 to 40 years. You never do anything. You talk about it, but you never come up with the "public share" in your community."

A whole group of us, in 1991 or 1992, went to San Antonio to learn how they restored their river. It was literally a trickle in a red light district. It wasn't a raging river. A group of women started the plan in San Antonio. They talked their husbands into buying ratty old buildings and putting consortiums together to repurchase down-town. Those are now, of course, Hilton Hotels and Hyatt Regencies, and all these people are very rich. They were very smart. But they were visionaries. They said, "We need to improve this. We need to make this river project work." The project in San Antonio actually started as a federal project in the 20s and has different segments. If you look at the river—if you walk along riverwalk, you can see the 20's, and the 30's and 40's, and the 50's and 60's architecture.

We sat down with some of the original women who helped put this together, who were, at this time, little old ladies in their mid-80s. We were all sitting at a table with powerful people who had worked on this project over the years. One wonderful woman turned around to all of us. I'll never forget this. She said, "You know, I've been to the Napa Valley several times. You're beautiful. You have every gift imaginable. We didn't have that. But, do you know what we had, that you don't seem to have?" She said, "The two things that we had that were the most important were vision and leadership." We sucked in our breath. It was like she had said, "You're really ugly! And stupid too!" It was so profound and so true. The two components we were missing were vision and leadership.

It was true. It hurt, but it was true. She didn't mean it like that. She was an 85-year-old woman and she was just stating a fact. This was like saying, "Your baby is ugly." She wasn't trying to say that. She was just telling us the truth. "You don't have any vision. You don't have any leadership. You're never going to get there."

That was the beginning spark. OK, who else is going to do it? If you don't do it, and if he doesn't do it, and if she doesn't do it . . . if we don't get together—and if somebody doesn't take the lead in making sure that the implementation of ideas occurs, it simply won't happen. We came back from San Antonio determined that we were going to find out how to make the city of Napa work, and how to work with the river.

So, we go through the devastating floods on the 10th of January and the 10th of March in 1995, and the Army Corps of Engineers comes back to us. They have several meetings in the county. They go to City Hall in Napa. They show their plan. They say, "Have we got a deal for you! We're going to fix your river, and we're going to do it like this: Big walls. Steel and rebar. We're going to do all these wonderful things." And a very funny city councilwoman at the time, Cindy Waters, said, "This looks like a gulag! We're not going to let this happen in our town! This is really ugly! We're not going to go for this!" The Army Corps of Engineers guys were saying, "That's it! You guys are flakes. We're not coming back. You guys never like what we're doing." The leaders who had fought to get flood control back were saying, "Oh, my god! What are we going to do now? The environmentalists and all the other folks hate this, but we've got to figure out how to stop the flooding." So it looked like the plan was dead. Everybody hated the flood control plan. Big articles in the newspaper: ARMY CORPS OF ENGINEERS SUCKS. They're terrible; they can't design anything! So a whole group of us got together and said, "We've got to figure this out. We have to deal with the flooding. Otherwise, it's going to destroy the Napa Valley. If we don't do something, the city of Napa will permanently stay in a 1950's timewarp."

By this time, Bill Clinton was in the White House. He was saying to the Army Corps of Engineers, for the first time ever, "I want you guys to look at creatively managing rivers instead of controlling them." The Corps said, "What do you mean, manage a river? I mean, we like rebar and steel. We've been doing this for 100 years. Who is this wacky guy telling us to manage rivers and be ecological and watch how they flow? This guy is nuts! But, he's the President, so we've got to do it." This thinking became a paradigm shift: "Thou shalt not dam up rivers. Thou shalt look at them and look at how they flow." These guys at the top didn't like it. It was very new thinking in the early 1990s for the Army Corps of Engineers, and they weren't ready for it.

A local author, Moira Johnston Block, was very interested in the river, so she and I formed a group called Friends of the River. This group was formed to raise the consciousness of the importance of the Napa River. It needed to be broad-based. We needed to invite everyone. We wanted hundreds of people to contribute to Friends of the River. And we would culminate the year's activities of education by hosting a wonderful concert on the river on Labor Day. The idea was to raise the local consciousness about how important the river is. It was wonderful and beautiful. Six thousand people would sit downtown on the banks of the river and listen to this concert. As the Friends of the River group got more involved in the flood control project, Moira became the voice for the river and the ecological sense of the river. She started reading every book she could get her hands on and talking to anyone she could about different methods for flood management.

We got a copy of the federal mandate for the Corps, their little bible. "Thou shalt not dam up rivers. Thou shalt look at them and look at how they flow." We read that and said, "Wait a minute. These guys are supposed to go in a different direction." They weren't going to tell us that.

So, when the Army Corps came in with another ugly plan in the mid-90s, the City Council in Napa went ballistic: "We hate it. It's a gulag. It will never be built." It looks like the river will die. We're never going to get flood control. The Corps will not bend. Since Moira had the new mandate, she went to the Corps management in Sacramento and said, "Wait a minute. It says right here you're not supposed to do it the old way." They say, "That's just the material from Washington. It doesn't filter down to us in the office in Sacramento!" Again, it looked like flood control was going to die entirely.

The county of Napa, however, had the most amazing guy, Dave Dickson. He's a real visionary. He's a worker. He's brilliant. He's a listener and he's creative. He understood what we had to do. We had to force the Army Corps of Engineers into understanding that we cannot do their plan, that the community must be involved. We needed to craft a community coalition that would get everybody involved, because the reason flood control had not passed in the past was that it was designed primarily for the city of Napa. St. Helena and Calistoga and Yountville didn't give a rip. They're saying, "What's in it for me?" And there's nothing. So they didn't vote for it. Now we needed a two-thirds vote, which was going to be nearly impossible to do. We had to raise the community's consciousness. We had to educate people. We had never done that before.

Dave Dickson said, "Let's find some county money. Let's find the best facilitators, and let's invite the entire community to be a part of this process." So we did. We invited 300 people: all the mayors of all the cities, the city managers of all the cities, the environmental community, the development community, and everybody in between. All the big projects, too. They were invited to sit in this big room that we had with tables all over, with their names in front of them, with a very professional, but corny, very well-planned facilitation of "How do we craft this plan and make it wonderful?" It only took a few meetings. In the first meeting, people said, "Wow! We're in control of our destiny! We can design this any way we want to! And then we'll figure out how to get the money." We brought in some of the most wonderful river experts from all over the world, who couldn't wait to get their hands on Napa. . . . And the process began. Over two years, we had meetings once a month—at the fairgrounds—with the community redesigning the river.

The Army Corps of Engineers came in with a lot of trepidation in the beginning. They were young. Moira and I got together and said, "These guys are lonely. They're single. I know how we can do this! We'll fix them up! We'll get them dates! We'll mommy them!" So we decided that we'd mother the Army Corps of Engineers. We would take care of them. I'd hug them and take them out to dinner and take them out to lunch and introduce them to cute, local river-conscious girls. And it worked. We were sure that some of the Corps members thought, "These women are nuts, but we don't know that we can get around this." As a group, we started saying, "We really need to make sure that this project is what the community wants, or we'll never get it passed." So we started talking about that. And they started to get it.

Then Moira—a touch of genius—said to them, in essence, "I could make your lives miserable. I'm very eloquent. I can stand in front of Congress and go on and on for hours and tell them how wonderful this river is, and how we want to do it the right way, and you won't do it the right way. Now, I can do that, or you can go along with me and all my friends, and we can try doing this cooperatively, with the community. Then, you will be heroes." A couple of us said, "Look—you guys will get big raises. You'll be well known. It will work. Trust us. You've got to design this project through the community process. We'll make sure.that it works from your standpoint, from an engineering standpoint, but you're going to have to go along with the community process."

We brought the head of the Army Corps of Engineers out here and took him on our boat trip down the Napa River. Every other weekend, we were on boat trips, dragging dignitaries along and educating them about the river by saying , "Did you know this?" We had the whole script down by heart. "Here are the Wappos. . . . Here are General Vallejo and his family." And we'd take all these folks down, and we'd talk about the possibilities of restoring the river ecologically and naturally. The head of the Army Corps of Engineers understood. He started figuring it out: "It could actually work—to my benefit. Everybody's looking at us now and saying, 'Hey, the finger-in-the-dike theory is a flop. You guys don't know what you're doing.' If this works here—Bingo! This is really going to give us some power. And if we don't do something pretty glamorous and sexy, nobody's going to care about the Army Corps of Engineers, because the Mississippi was a dismal failure." So the timing was perfect. Here's this valley that everybody knows about. Here's this community coalition process with 300 people. This was what they were supposed to do. The light went on. This might just work!

We took what the Army Corps of Engineers originally designed, crunched it up into a ball, tossed it in the toilet, and redesigned the entire river, with experts—great experts from all over the world. It took two years. The community had taken over. And the Corps of Engineers went back to Sacramento with a deep sigh, saying, "These people are nuts, especially the women!" But it's beginning to take some real form. People are having fun with it. Writers are coming in and watching the process of building consensus, of understanding that difficult "C" word—Compromise. It was the most amazing thing I'd ever seen in my life.

It was an absolutely perfect example of the way to solve community issues: form a coalition process. Get everyone with all their divergent views together, stick them in a room, lock the doors, and make them figure out a solution. There are partisan voices on either side of any issue who only understand and hear their own point of view and do not understand the whole, but they will either have to understand the whole, because it will be drummed into them over and over again, or they will have no power. And the group will begin to take on a life of its own. The path is easily carved. That's what happened.

I loved watching people come up with their own answers, watching shy people stand up in a group and say, "I'd like to see this happen," and feeling this enormous sense of pride when everybody

turns around and says, "Wow! Great idea!" Watching the selfish people who just wanted to be listened to in public get shut down. It's the
most amazing thing. It became the strong arms of everyone enfolding
one another and creating an overwhelming wave of creativity and
problem solving. None of these problems were that difficult, but you'd
think in many communities they would be, because people don't solve
them. They do not create the stage for creative problem solving and
consensus building in community. When you have communities with
people who understand how to build consensus, it works.

We reached consensus on the plan, and it was wonderful: by
restoring the river as it once was, widening the areas that were too
narrow and fixing the oxbow, by creating a wet-dry bypass that will
become a public festival site where we will do wonderful concerts in
the future, and by creating a beautiful public park. As we designed the
perfect plan, the price jacked up to $180 million. Again, half of it
would be paid for by the federal government. Half of it, we would
have to come up with locally. So we went from designing the river
into the campaign of our lives. It was a political campaign and a
vote that most people said would never pass.

There was less than a year before the election. Not even a year!
We had about eight months to accomplish a miracle. A few of us
became the lead team on a Measure A campaign and asked, "How are
we going to pull this sucker off? What's it going to take?" We started
out looking for a firm that had an ability to pull off these kinds of
difficult political campaigns, and we found a wonderful woman in
San Francisco who had designed several successful campaigns and
really met our needs, really understood who we were, and wanted to
work with us. We started putting a budget together for what this
campaign would take, to make sure that we could create materials that
were good, that might be expensive but didn't look expensive, yet were
very thorough. We needed volunteers to walk neighborhoods, walk
precincts, knock on doors, stand in front of Target on weekends—do
the guerrilla marketing that would bring us success!

The volunteers for Measure A were a mixture of environmentalists and business people, and, for the first time in history, the
National Sierra Club endorsed our flood control plan. The National
Sierra Club endorsing an Army Corps of Engineers project was
unheard of. That's a coalition process!

March 3, 1998 was the vote. It passed by a margin of 314 votes. But it passed.

The night it passed, all of us were at the Town Center. We made crowns for everybody. Bob and Margrit were there. All of us were there, a mixed crowd of everyone was there. And what magic Napa, the city, will experience! Seven bridges will be rebuilt. Big, huge earthmoving equipment will move into the cities and county. Streets will be closed. The theme song for the city of Napa for five years will be Dust, Dust, and More Dust. Everybody will complain! People will see old buildings removed, wrecking balls will knock stuff down; stuff will go up. Massive change. Which is what is needed. But massive change in a city that has never liked even itsy bitsy changes. The whole valley will change, but the city of Napa will change the most. It will come into its own and be reborn!

That's where we are now in our story. We need to preserve the Napa Valley. We have pledged that we will continue with the process of working way outside the box, being amazingly committed, and being really creative, and doing it through a community process of coming up with wonderful concepts that haven't been done before.

Measure A and Communication

by Ron Birtcher

The success of the Napa River Restoration Movement—the Measure A success—really came from the community. Dana Leavitt, Dorothy Lind, and their committee spent an enormous amount of time organizing the amalgamation of several different forces in conjunction with the city/county. They were able to do it without government endorsement, and yet to marry the needs of the city and the county as well as the federal government, and then also marry Up Valley and Down Valley. It really is a relationship issue between Up Valley and Down Valley as much as it is a flood control issue. Somewhere, a long time ago, the Wappo Indians drew a line, I guess, or somebody did, and said, "We live Up Valley; you live Down Valley." And that has had a very significant negative impact on getting people together to think in terms of a united Napa Valley.

The flood control issue failed twice. Measure A was the third try at it. There were some very significant evaluations as to why it failed. It was basically communication, as is usually the case. No matter what side of any issue you're on, it either succeeds or fails because one side has the communicator who can articulate the issues well, so that people can make up their mind. One side has the ability to lay out the situation much better than the other.

This had to be communicated: the people in this valley had to understand that this may be our last chance of getting some kind of significant federal government support before it dries up and goes away, or we're going to pay this price forever and ever and ever. And the price is quite dear. Not just the price of the sandbags, but the price of the loss of business, and the price of decreased valuation of properties. The value of properties up and down the river—what it costs all the way from Napa clear up to Calistoga. When they talk about Napa River flooding, everybody thinks in terms of downtown Napa, because that's where the pictures are taken. The water coming up to the bridge. But the reality is there are a whole lot of places for thirty miles on this river that are affected by it. So the recognition of the importance of this really became paramount.

It failed once. Why did it fail? Communication. We didn't have enough money to get out there and talk about the issues—try to "over-talk," if you will, the anti-movement. It's so easy to vote No and so difficult to vote Yes—especially when it's involving money. It's always easier to vote No anyway, because a No vote will let you off the hook when you don't understand. So if you don't understand or care to do the research, you vote No. You vote for the status quo. It's nonrisk.

Measure A required a Yes vote. So it was very important that the knowledge be out there—and not just knowledge of what the ad said in the newspaper or what the editorial said or what was being espoused on the local radio—but talking eye to eye. "Let's understand what's going on in your backyard and my backyard." If I were to go to your home, you'd tell me, "I don't live in Napa. And I don't have a business down there. My barbershop doesn't get wet. So I don't really care about *your* problems." It was difficult to try to convince everybody. It had to be all the voters of the uplands as well. They had to understand what it really meant to the valley.

Dorothy Lind used the Roundtable concept at the Fair. She coordinated a 300-member, communitywide group. She organized meetings to bring together different groups to talk about the issues. As many groups as you possibly can, all in the same room, all trying to understand what the consequences were if this failed. And what the consequences were within the valley.

Dorothy and a few significant others, tenaciously putting in 29 hours a day for months, pulled this thing off, with raising money, with going to several of the big winery operators here and getting significant dollars Up Valley. They got people to recognize the importance of the river to the community as a whole.

With the big donors, there wasn't a drop of water that ever touched their properties, ever touched their vineyards at any time during any of the floods. There really had to be some significant dollars—$25,000 and $50,000 and $75,000 at a pop. So why did they give?

The river is a very significant part of our life. It isn't just an environmental issue. It isn't just a fish issue or a frog that may disappear or a tadpole. It really is a basis for saying the river is the community, and it's always going to be here. And it's bigger than us. Either we've got to fix it or we're going to pay the consequences. It was a very close vote. A very, very close vote. But it did pass.

Just the word "change" makes shivers go up and down everybody. Either you shiver with excitement—finally you're going to change something—or you shiver with fear—you're going to change something I've become very accustomed to. So, the word "change" in anybody's vernacular causes all kinds of emotion. It doesn't necessarily mean that they're unified, but they all are excited about the change. Whether or not it ever comes up to the front depends upon whether the Changer or the Changee is motivated to fight, to defend or push forward—or whatever their cause may be. From that comes this pull and tug and pull and tug. There's overreaction on everybody's side. There comes the politics of it all. Slowly, the issues get brought up before a council of some sort—the planning commission or the city council or a state legislature or the county board of supervisors or just a new little group. Somebody has to get people together.

II
The
Residents

Immigrants

by Jamie Davies

It all started when my husband Jack came to me and said he'd
like to quit his job and start a business. He said he'd like me to be his
partner! Of course, I was eager to do it and flattered that he wanted
me as his business partner. In the 60s it was rare for a woman to be
in business. We started daydreaming about the opportunities available
to us. I had owned an art gallery in San Francisco and was beginning a
new family in Los Angeles where Jack's company was based. I thought
the art world was where I could make the best contribution. Jack
was a very talented and creative businessman. I knew our combined
talents would work for us as a business team.

We went through the list of creative endeavors. My art business—
I knew he wouldn't want to be involved in that. Fine books, music,
theater—there was no way for us to make a living in these areas. We
kept thinking about our mutual love for entertaining, the joy of bringing people together over food and wine, including wines from Napa
County. Jack and I had always enjoyed the Napa experience. We felt
a sense of belonging. We thought it was a great place in terms of its
natural beauty and human qualities. We wanted to be part of it and
raise our family here. We thought it would be wonderful to contribute
something to the community, to add a bit of ourselves to the place.

So we began looking for a vineyard and winery. At the end of a
long search, we found the historic Schram property on this wooded
mountain and moved into the derelict Victorian. Getting to know our
neighbors was easy. In our case, however, they were worried that we
might be relations of the former owner, who hadn't paid her bills. It
was also difficult to transcend the "city slickers" brand they saw

emblazoned on our foreheads. We had to prove that we were dedicated to making world-class champagne at Schramsberg. The seriousness of our commitment became evident to the old timers quickly and they moved to support us.

At the time we left Los Angeles that city was undergoing what some liked to call "progress." The historic buildings were being torn down to make room for strip malls and housing developments. We were eager to escape this mentality, to settle in a place where it was possible to live in harmony with the land.

Coming from LA, we were familiar with growth, high-density residential neighborhoods, rapid commercialization, industrialization, and, of course, the freeways. We knew that the Santa Clara Valley, which had been agricultural for many years, and was known for its beautiful fruit trees, olive groves, and vineyards, was rapidly being transformed into Silicon Valley. Some of these same changes had begun happening in the city of Napa. The old Victorians and buildings along the river from the 1800s were being replaced by cinder block and built-up concrete buildings. There was no heart or art to this.

At the same time, there were people in the valley who did have a respect for heritage, history, and preservation. Jack and I wanted to be among those people who were trying to retain the heritage by rebuilding, not destroying, that past. It would have been easy for someone to come in and buy Schramsberg—the property we purchased—dismantle it and turn it into something modern and sterile. We wanted to revive this historic property so that future generations would be able to see what it was like 100 years ago when winemaking first took place in this valley. We also wanted to help rebuild the reputation Napa had enjoyed as a premium wine-growing region prior to prohibition. We felt very strongly about protecting the land for agriculture and joining forces with other people in the county to accomplish this goal.

Our arrival in the valley coincided with the Board of Supervisors' rethinking the land-use policies for Napa County. The prior board had adopted a fast-growth policy, which included the adoption of a freeway route right through the middle of the valley. Cal Trans (the California Department of Transportation) had already acquired property in order to make that possible. We saw this as a serious threat to the preservation of agricultural land throughout the area. If the prior board's wishes had come true, there would have been rotating 76 signs and Burger Kings lining the valley's main arterial. The land would have been subdivided in a short time. People were forecasting houses as the last crop for this fertile farming region. The new Board of Supervisors was taking a hard look at the long-range versus short-range goals for land use in the valley. They were considering agriculture as the highest use for the land. The voice coming out of the supervisors' office seemed to be saying, "This is a small place. Let's emphasize our exclusive qualities and the character of this region. We can make Napa County an exception and set an example for other regions on how to retain agricultural land without stifling the vitality of neighboring cities." The new supervisors began working on the Agricultural Preserve (AP) concept. The conviction supporting the Ag Preserve was that agriculture is, and should continue to be, the predominant use of the valley floor and foothills areas of Napa County. Further, a zoning ordinance was proposed that increased the minimum parcel size from one acre to twenty acres on the valley floor, with larger parcels required on the hillsides. Jack and I were eager to help establish this AP plan.

There had been a great deal of press about the rapid growth occurring in the Santa Clara Valley. By some accounts it was considered the second richest agricultural area in the country, and it was being totally paved over. That stimulated a great deal of interest in conservation and environmental issues throughout the nine Bay Area counties. The environmentalists, then, like now, were considered by some to be rabid, crazy people, but others felt that we should be heard. As I recall, it was the Save the Earth group that was taking an active role. One evening we attended a meeting at the home of Dorothy Erskine. That's when Jack was tapped as the chairman of the citizens committee to help the Board of Supervisors establish the Ag Preserve. He accepted gladly because he felt that he could make a difference.

Jack chaired the citizens committee, bringing more and more support for the AP concept that was being prepared by the Planning Commission and the Board of Supervisors. Other organizations and individuals throughout the county were also at work supporting the plan. The members of the Planning Commission and the Board of Supervisors had put their own political lives on the line. They were under attack by some of their constituents who opposed the changes being proposed. Fortunately, they not only believed in what they were doing, they were passionate about it.

During this time the city and county officials were asking for grass roots support. That brought a mixed bag of people together to work on a common cause: the farmer, the plumber, the policeman, the butcher, the schoolteacher, each with their own view on the matter. This group represented a broad spectrum of the community. The fight for the Agricultural Preserve was not confined to newcomers. The issue pulled in people from everywhere. Without this support, the supervisors would have been unable to proceed.

Some long-term vintners and residents were very upset at the thought of restrictions on what they could do with their private property. This is where we ran head-to-head with a lot of our neighbors who had lived in this area all their lives. Many had parents who came here at an early age. They wanted the option to sell their land or divide it into mini-parcels so that each member of the family could have his or her own space. But theirs was a short-term, not a long-term view, of future land use. They had their own leaders to represent them at the many public hearings that took place before the County Commissioners and the Board of Supervisors. These meetings were long with much heated debate between unhappy property owners.

It took two years to establish the Napa County Agricultural Preserve. During that time friends were pitted against friends, old timers against old timers, families against families. There were a lot of hard feelings at the end of it all. Some people never spoke to each other again. Over time, many of those who had openly opposed the Ag Preserve came to us and said, "We were wrong. The Ag Preserve was the best way to save our valley." It was difficult to build consensus among the conservative farmers and residents, but in the end one has to make a choice: either you self-regulate or allow individuals to have their own way and destroy the culture you are trying to save.

After the Agricultural Preserve was put into effect in 1968, the next step was to stop the freeway plan. Members of the community went to our state senator, Peter Behr from Marin County, and asked him to present a bill at the state legislature to delete the freeway from the Cal Trans program. Peter Behr was a believer and well regarded in Sacramento, so he was more than happy to present the bill. But he had to get votes. He needed citizens to go to the state capitol and impress upon the state legislature and the assembly that this was the right thing to do. At that time people were beginning to question the need for so many freeways in the state. If you take a marvelous region like Napa and cover it in asphalt, it's gone forever.

We went to Sacramento to speak with representatives of Cal Trans. We wanted to know, from the source, what the real plan for this freeway was. Through these discussions we discovered that the plan wasn't fully determined. Funds were available to build a freeway and they had to spend the money within a specified period of time. They were talking about boring a tunnel through Mt. St. Helena to Lake County, and from there they couldn't say. There had been some talk about an alternate route to 101 as well. This made the citizens in the area uneasy, they didn't want anything to do with it. In the end we were able to defeat the project.

Subsequently, the concept of the Ag Preserve has been challenged many times, but has always been upheld. In one instance, enough citizens were concerned about upholding the laws established by the AP that they formed a new community action group that proposed Measure J (or Bill 2020). The Bill passed, limiting the power of the city and county officials to make exceptions to the AP zoning law. Any proposed exception has to be put to a vote of the general population. The measure strengthened the protection of agricultural lands until the year 2020. While the system is working, we must remain watchful of what happens in 2020 when the measure expires.

What's critical now, as always, is the need to educate people as to the intent of the Ag Preserve and the citizens' responsibility to maintain the agricultural system. It is easy to forget that there are new residents and second-generation residents who need to know that the quality of life here, that some take for granted, wouldn't exist if not for the Ag Preserve. We all have an obligation to participate in understanding it and contributing to the long-range goal. It's challenging. The Agricultural Preserve has provided us a unique opportunity to continue the agricultural legacy we have inherited by assuming the responsibility of caretakers. It is challenging; developers are constantly at our heels trying to get a foot in the door. The development south of Napa is going to have a big impact on the community that we hold dear. We need votes to uphold the agricultural land policies.

We are a community that has the ability to make a difference. People here are devoted to this land, and not only for greed or the need to exchange dollars. They come, as we did, because there is something inherently beautiful, compelling, heartwarming, and life fulfilling about being here. It doesn't matter if you live in a tent, a Victorian, a castle, or a boat. We are all in this together and must follow our passion for what is right and true for the Napa Valley. It will be up to us to carry on the legacy that was started by those who came before us.

Working the Vines

by Jaime Aguirre

*Most of the books that have been written about Napa are
about winery principals. Because the Hispanic population is
really the backbone of the industry, in terms of the labor force,
it would be unthinkable to write a story about Napa as a
community without including all of us. We wouldn't be here
without the workers and vice versa. We are co-dependent.
We are brought together not only in the workplace but in the
schools and in the church, and in every other walk of life. In
order to exist in a community, we have to interact. Jaime
Aguirre has been our vineyard manager at Schramsberg for
over 30 years.*

—Jamie Davies

My father came here as a Bracero. (During World War II,
California encouraged Mexican workers to come to the United States
as fieldworkers in a program called the Bracero Program.) Around
1941–1942, he worked in the Yolo area, and he came to the Napa
area to visit. He liked the Napa Valley, so he found a job after he
finished his contract as a Bracero. Later he came here on his own
and stayed here. When I was seven years old, he sent for my mother,
my two sisters, my two brothers, and me.

When we started working here, there were very few Hispanic
families in the Napa Valley. I would say we knew every family. The
oldest families that I remember: the Espinosas have been in St. Helena
for many, many years; the Escareños—another big family; the Perez's
still live here in St. Helena; and the Aguirres—which is us. During
harvest time, these families used to work all the harvests. At that

39

time, not much ground was developed. Carneros were just hills. Pope
Valley was undeveloped. Here in Napa Valley there were walnuts,
prunes, grapes, and a little bit of pears. There were not that many
grapes at that time. The families would get everything done here, and
then move on to other harvests.

We used to start in Sebastopol with the apples, and then move
on to the grapes. And then to Madera for the cotton. We just kept
moving around, and during pruning, we'd come back to do the pruning. We would start in Fairfield, pruning the apricots, peaches, and
pears. We'd get done with them, and go to Sebastopol right after
that. We'd pick the apples in Sebastopol, and then we'd move out to
pick cotton.

Back then, it was the whole family that worked. In my wife's
family, when her brother Mike was a little boy, they had him out in
the field. They were babysitting and working at the same time. The
mothers would take breaks and feed the children, and go back. I was
only seven, but I worked with my parents from 6:30 in the morning
until dark, because back then there was no 8-hour day.

It was pretty hard to go to school because we were moving
around so much. I learned how to read, how to do a little math, at
home, with my sisters. I went to school here, but I just went one
year. When I was in third grade; they figured out I knew how to read
and how to add and multiply, and I went through a little test, and
passed to the fourth grade in one year.

My wife Teresa went to high school here. The way they worked,
they would get up at five o'clock in the morning and go to the fields.
From the fields, they would take their clothes to go to school. From
school, they would go back to the fields until dark. Homework was
done and they had to be in bed by eight o'clock or 8:30 to get ready
for the next day. That was the routine of the Hispanic families.

When we moved around, they had little shacks for the workers,
just temporary. Here in Rutherford, they had an abandoned school.
It was big, and all the workers lived there during the picking season.
We had a house that we were renting—our base home—on Whitehall
Lane. But when we worked in Sebastopol, they would provide us
with temporary places.

We didn't have papers back then, so my parents had in their
mind that we were not going to be here for too long, so take advantage
of the work available. There were no 8-hour days or 40-hour weeks.

It was just work, work, work, work. Every day. Through harvest, you don't have even Sundays off. Even now, you work straight through.

We were here for three years, and then Immigration sent us back. It's not like we wanted to go back. When we went back, I was ten years old, and I started going to school in Mexico. After six years, we came back, and at that time, I met Teresa.

When I came back here, I didn't go to school. It was pretty hard for me to move back and forth. I kind of learned the system in Mexico, and I was doing pretty well. But when I came here and went to summer school, it was not easy, because I had forgotten the English that I had learned before, and they didn't have any tutors then. They sent us to the library, and everyone had to explain a story that we had to read. I got so embarrassed, I said, "Well, if I don't have help, I don't feel that I can be in school." So I decided I'm going to work. I was only 16. I got a permit from school to work, and I started working for Christian Brothers which was right across the road from Schramsberg at that time. It was vineyard work. It was pretty hard—I didn't have quite the strength to work as an adult back then—but I had to keep up in order to keep the job.

Otherwise, I had to go back to school. I don't think I would have gone back anyway, because it was embarrassing. You'd sit there and not know what they were telling you or what you're supposed to be doing. There was no one to help you with the language. So I worked for Christian Brothers for a while. A few years later, I started working for Beaulieu Vineyards for a few years.

Later I was recommended to Schramsberg. Mr. Davies and Andre Tschelicheff worked it out. Andre was the superintendent at Beaulieu. Mr. Davies told Andre that he needed a foreman. They wanted me to be foreman. I thought at the time—I'm too young. (I was 21 years old. I was married and had two children then.) I told him, "You have other people there with more years, more age, more experience, more knowledge." But they thought that I had learned enough to be a foreman, so they said, "Why don't you go and try. We're pretty sure you can do it. And if you don't make it, well, you just come back and you have your job." "OK," I said, "but if I don't make it, I'd like to have my job back." And now I'm still here. And I'm happy.

We have three children—one boy and two girls. When I was younger, I played soccer for many, many years. I stopped playing soccer when our kids started playing sports in school. We would go and watch all of their football, volleyball, baseball, and softball games. Now, we form part of the choir in the Calistoga Catholic Church. I teach the new kids how to play the guitar. That is my pastime. We are committed to our church; we play at the Spanish Mass on Saturday evenings. My son and I play the guitar, and Teresa and Norma, my daughter-in-law, sing. The grandchildren also like to sing with us. And sometimes we sing at social events.

When I first met Teresa, it's kind of interesting, because she didn't know Spanish. In her house, her father had to learn English in order to keep his job. So they were not allowed to speak Spanish at home. When I met her, she could not speak Spanish, and I could not speak that much English, so we used our own sign language. She went to school in St. Helena High School up to the twelfth grade. Once we got married, we both worked.

At one time we worked the vineyards together. She was the fastest woman in her crew. My supervisor thought that I was cheating and helping her out, so they moved her to a different crew. She was not worried. She beat every man and woman in that crew too! She worked in various orchards—pear, apple, apricots, peaches. She also has picked tomatoes, prunes, and walnuts. She worked on the bottling lines for various wineries. She's been with Sutter Home for the last 19 years. She developed spasms in her arm and the doctor restricted that type of work. Because of her hard work, Sutter Home provided Teresa with lighter duty; she works at the security gate at Sutter Home. In the harvest, she is the Weigh Master. During harvest, she works up to 14 hours a day. We are very happy that Sutter Home gave her that position. The Trinchero family are very nice people. With her help, with us both working, we have been able to send our kids to college.

Now, my children are wearing my shoes. My son, Jimmy, understands the reasons we did what we did to discipline and educate them. He now sees it with his children, Angelica and Daniella. Connie's daughters, Elizabeth and Jacqueline, are going to St. John's Catholic School. She and her husband Juan say it's a sacrifice keeping them in private school, but it's worth the effort.

Sometimes, the young kids say, "Well, I go to school, but I'm not sure what I want to be, what I want to do." At the beginning, I didn't have a choice, but I had to make it work, so now I enjoy it. I think that you need to make goals. Nothing is easy. Nothing comes to you. You have to go to it.

It is important to go to school and get an education, so that we do not have to do the work in the fields. I think it's very important to transmit to the children your thoughts, good or bad, just so they can learn, and so they do not make the mistakes that you've made. That is why communication is very important. Let's not make the same mistakes twice. Mistakes can stop you from growing.

Our oldest boy, Jimmy, learned to work here in the vineyards. I thought he was going to continue to work in the vineyards. He went to work for Sterling for a short time. They offered him a full-time job, but then something happened to the position. So he went to work in construction and joined the union. Construction went down, so he started working for Far Niente. Within a year he took the title of cellarmaster. He later got married, and now he's working for Sutter Home. His mind is always thinking to go one step a little higher. He had an interview at Sutter Home—they asked him, "Why are you trying to change jobs?" He said, "Well, this is a bigger company. I'd like to have more experience, just to learn a little more and grow." So they gave him the opportunity. He's been there since August, and he's very happy. He has a chance to learn how to run the bottling lines. They're training him to be an operator in the cellar.

Our daughter Connie also works in the valley. After she finished high school, she went to college in Sacramento. Now she works for the county of Napa, at Social Services, as a fraud investigator for welfare. Connie's husband, Juan Roldan, works for Far Niente Winery as their maintenance manager.

My youngest daughter Patty attended Sacramento State. She worked for Express Personnel here in Napa. It's an employment agency. She would interview the employees. They hire people and then send them out to work. She is now working as an eligibility worker at Napa County.

My children have stayed in the valley. I think it's the family that keeps us together. Our youngest daughter, she was going to move to Sacramento. Her husband, Kelly Hull (her boyfriend then), was in Memphis. So she went to visit Memphis, and she said, "I would go to Sacramento, but I would not go to Memphis. It's too far. I want to be close to home." So she started to work for Express Personnel. Before she got married, her fiance came here, and she found him a job. That's how he stayed here. He likes it. He's really happy about it. His feeling is that it is different, being part of an Hispanic family, but he tries everything! We have a different way of doing things. We are very united. Our children still call us for advice. Our children will call family for childcare before finding childcare that is not related. The kids call each other at least four times a week.

In the beginning, we'd say, "Some day, we'll retire to Mexico." Now, I don't think so, because the family is growing. I don't think we could stay too far from them. We've gotten used to being together.

For Teresa, Spanish is almost a second language. She used to be afraid that she would not speak Spanish correctly—that sometimes she's not saying the right word or the right sentence. Our children use both languages at work. They are practicing all the time. Both languages are *part* of their work. The first generation American-Mexicans are bilingual for the most part. I think that most Hispanics would like to learn English if they had the opportunity. Our grandchildren have all spoken Spanish first and began learning English once they went to pre-school. That is our tradition, our culture. It is easy to forget Spanish if you are speaking in English all of the time. Our children also spoke Spanish mostly before they went to kindergarten. We would take them to Mexico every year since they were very little. We wanted them to know where we came from, where our roots are, and how we got here. Now, as adults they go back to Mexico with their families. As for myself, I watch TV, and the whole time I am translating from English to Spanish. Sometimes I lose track, because it doesn't match what I'm trying to put together. When I'm speaking to someone— sometimes I say, "Explain a little different way, so I can understand."

Once, we had a school bus with computers. They would come out here two times a week, and we were learning a lot of things on the computers. I had never touched a computer until then. Some of the students in the beginning could not speak more than two words in English. Some of these students understood the words, but were embarrassed to say them out loud. After a few of the classes, they began saying the words out loud. Finally, they were saying, "Good morning. How are you?" "Thank you." And moving along. I feel that was a big benefit.

We also worked on math. I was much better at math in school, and when the school bus was here, I was able to work on problems that I had forgotten how to do. I feel that the school bus program should have continued. It was making a big difference. I guess there was not enough money to continue with the program.

Now they are saying that they do not want to teach any more Spanish, because English is the Number One language and they want everyone to learn it. I agree that everyone should understand and speak English because it is very important to be able to communicate with the whole community. We need more teachers helping students out in the beginning, in their language, saying, "OK, you said it wrong. This is a table. It's a mesa." So that the student understands what they are saying. Something to get them started. I think that at the beginning, it's important. If they don't understand the language and somebody speaks to them, they feel like they don't belong there. That's the way I felt in school. That's why I think it's very hard.

I've been working at Schramsberg since the first of March, 1968, over 30 years. It is surprising that the years have gone by so fast. When I first came here, the operation was much smaller, and everything was much harder to do. Everything was done by hand. During crush, I would work from 8:00 A.M. until 2:00–3:00 A.M. the next morning. I did all the filtration and racking and pressing and the vineyard. We only had the lower vineyard. Then we started developing the upper vineyard and everything started growing. Now, it's still long hours, but we have machines that do most of the hard work.

I find other people to work just by word. I asked the people who have already worked. They've been around. Every year through harvest, we have different people. Normally, they're local, so I can give them a call, and they know somebody else. That's how we get our people. There is also cooperation with those we know; for example, I can call my brother-in-law for workers during harvest if I can't find anyone.

Last year, I asked Fred, who is the financial administrator here, "Fred, are you willing to help us pick grapes for a little bit, just so you see what it's like?" I told him, "It's hard work out there. You guys work here in front of the computer, and the computer is telling you what and when, what time, how much, everything, but that's just one part. It would be nice for you to have just a little taste of the other part, so at least you have an inside feeling of what it takes to do the other half."

He said, "Sure, sure, sure." He went out there. He said, "My god, I don't believe how these guys do it." He was impressed. It's a different ballgame. Now, at least, he knows what it's all about. He has an idea of it. We have to work together to make sure everything happens, so that we keep our jobs. It's nice to share and be aware of what's going there and what's going here—to get together and make things happen. I feel that it's so important for us who work on the vineyards, in the fields, because it's very hard work! Unfortunately, in some companies the hard work does not get recognized.

When I first came here, Mr. Davies and I started working together. I said to Mr. Davies, "I know that you're the owner here, but this is the way I was taught how to tie the vines and I can explain to you why they are tied this way." The next day, he was helping me to do some budding. I was watching him, and I said, "You know, that knife that you have there is not sharp." He said, "Yes, it's sharp. It's brand new." I said, "I know it's new, but it's not sharp enough." He was saying, "Yes, it's sharp!" So I said, "I will lend you my knife and then I will sharpen your knife. We'll change, just so you can see the difference." So he grabbed my knife and he cut his finger. He put it on the ground and he left. That was the end of budding for him.

One day he told me, "You know, I'm going to learn how to prune." "Sure. OK." "I'm going to go up there with you and I'm going to have gloves and pruning shears and all the gear and the system." He was pruning—and he was there for a good 15 minutes. Then he said, "I have to go and make a phone call. I'll be back." That was the end of his pruning. But that was what I was hired for. I feel very happy and proud of my job. Mr. Davies and I shared a great experience.

Working in the Cellar

by Ramon Viera

Ramon Viera is the Head Riddler for Schramsberg. Riddling, a skill unique to the preparation of champagne, involves turning each bottle slightly every day, to bring the yeast sediment down to the neck. The sediment will be "disgorged" from the bottle before the final cork is inserted. One of Ramon's leading roles is as ambassador. People love to watch the riddling. They're very interested in the process. And Ramon is a good teacher, so he gets to demonstrate his skills to people touring the winery. People love it. He has made quite a name for himself here.

—Jamie Davies

I came here in 1968 to visit a friend. He had already worked a few years here in the United States, and there was a good soccer team here. They invited me to come and join them. That's why I came to the United States. When I first came here, I came illegally. I worked for maybe four years, and then I fixed my visa. Now everybody is legal, because there was the amnesty. That helped a lot of people.

The soccer team was in St. Helena—the Napa Rangers. In 1970, we were the champions of northern California, and again in 1971. We didn't become professionals. We just played. In those days, half of the team worked for Schramsberg and the other half worked in St. Helena at Lambert's Chicken Farm. I began working at the farm in 1968. After returning to Mexico for a while, I came back here and found work at Schramsberg.

Starting in 1970, I worked for nine months part time. They hired me full time in 1976. In those days, we worked in both the vineyards and the winery. There was only Mr. Davies, Jaime, and Victor. They did everything. Then, Schramsberg started growing little by little, and they started to hire more people.

I learned to riddle when Mr. Davies and Jaime did it. Then in 1976, Efrén, Jorge, and I—we turned the bottles. I remember I started riddling 7,000 bottles. And then little by little, more and more and more, until now we riddle 50,000 bottles.

A lot of people think—did they send you to France to learn? I wish! We just learned from each other, and found the best and quickest way to turn the bottles. For some reason, my stations went a little faster or better. The touch has to be very soft. If you jerk the bottles or hit them too hard, the sediment moves and never settles. You have to be very quick and soft. That's how it works. I feel great knowing I am doing a good job.

I am the Head Riddler here at Schramsberg. A lot of people ask me if I have a big head because of that, but it's just like anything else. Everyone has their own abilities. This is a gift from God. I just learned riddling by working. Efrén and Jorge are quicker or faster than me, but my touch is the difference. I have to be grateful to God.

Maybe I am too comfortable with my job. I'm not very aggressive to look for something more. I don't want to try a different job. Maybe I'm afraid to try something else. What if I don't make it? I want to feel good about myself so I am not very adventurous. But I am proud of my work. That's why I said, "I want to work here." People ask me, "How many years have you been doing the same thing?" And I say, "A few years." "Do you get bored?" "No. I don't have time to get bored. I have to concentrate on whatever I'm doing."

We don't always know why things work. People ask, "Why did this one work? Why didn't this one work?" A lot of questions. I have to show the winemaker why. I put some bottles in one of the machines to find out how it will work. For him, it looks good. I have to show him why it isn't good. Then he starts to understand. You have to check very close. Right away, when I get a bottle after the riddling process, I can see if it is clear or not. Because all the time I have been working, I know.

In 1983, there was a little contest—there were eight people. We marked the bottles, and when you look at the marks, you see who has the best touch. I won the contest. One of them was a guy named Kent, from Domaine Chandon. He's the main guy there. He taught me a few things. When I started working here, they sent me there. He's quick also. Later, a couple of guys came here a few times from Domaine Chandon. Kent sent them to see me and see how we do it at Schramsberg. I heard them whisper, "He's like Kent." I said to myself, "I'm even better than him!"

I am my own boss here. Whatever I am doing here, there is nobody bothering me. I like my work. It's very interesting. Knowing and being a part of Schramsberg—I am proud to be here. It's very prestigious. Schramsberg is the best, and I feel great and am grateful to be here. They treat us like a family. That's the way we do things here.

As Head Riddler for Schramsberg, I have appeared in many articles and magazines. One of them was *LIFE* magazine in 1994. There was also a Mexican program in Florida. They came here and interviewed me. I was on TV in Mexico. When I went to Mexico next, a couple of friends told me, "We saw you on TV!" It was nice.

The soccer team was together until 1975. Then for some reason we split apart. We made two teams. Little by little, a couple of players would leave the team, until the Napa Rangers disappeared. For some reason, we stopped playing together. In those days, there were eight or nine teams, and we just split. But we still kick the ball around. And I helped for nine years in St. Helena with youth soccer.

After working hard, you relax a lot by running, concentrating, and playing soccer. You need to be in good condition, and you have to use your mind and your whole body. That's why we say that soccer is a complete sport. In soccer, you use your head, your chest, your legs, and everything—except your hands.

Now, a group of us who work for Schramsberg—most of us run. We have a nice place to practice up here. Some go out in the park at lunchtime. I go after work, myself. We encourage each other. Last year, if we made seven minutes a mile, we try to cut a little bit or at least keep that time. We start running with a big group. People push you. You don't want to fall behind. You keep pushing and pushing. Usually, that's how we finish. We don't try to be the first ones, but we try to make a good time.

My wife Isabel was born in Napa. When I met her, she barely spoke Spanish, and I didn't speak a word of English. I learned English from my wife, and by working here. I remember when Mr. Davies wanted one of us to learn a little English. Efrén and Jorge—they have one year more than me working here, but they only speak Spanish. I took some night classes, but only for a couple of years. I was learning quickly, but the more I learned, the harder it got.

Isabel and I have our own house in St. Helena. We have two children. My daughter Marisa just turned 26, and our son, Andres, is 22. Our daughter is still living with us, and our son is going to school in Oakland. He's studying to be an athletic trainer. He's taking psychology, sociology, and Spanish. He's going to be something better than us. My wife and myself, we have to work hard. We hope that he can go to school and do something better.

Our children went to the Catholic schools, because we thought they were better schools, very educational and disciplined. We always helped with their schools. Isabel was a coach for the girl's volleyball team for four years. We got involved in any sport to help.

My son started playing soccer with me when he was four or five years old, kicking the ball around. He learned to kick the ball back. He was an excellent soccer player, but he quit and decided to play basketball. Now he is going to school on a basketball scholarship. Andres thinks so positively. He always wanted to be the best. He worked 100 percent and put 100 percent effort into everything. He always told my mother and his cousins, "I want to be the first professional in the Viera family." We already have a couple of family members who have completed their college education. But he says, "I want to be better than everybody." We feel great about that.

I hope our children get a good education to be better. When they were growing up, education was the first thing. My father brought us up that way too. My parents told me to go to school and be better than them. Maybe I say the same thing. I was lucky. People trusted me. I have had only three jobs. I learned the jobs quickly and I always felt confident. My parents always encouraged me to be more responsible than other people. I taught that to my children too. I think it worked.

My son learned to do everything with me when he was little. I started paying him $3 per hour when he was 14–15 years old. I wanted to see him do things right. I told him, "Wherever you work, you can't do it sloppy and then come back and fix it the next day." That's the way my father taught me also. I don't want you to kill yourself, but I don't want you to just fool around either. This is the way you do it. I told my son and daughter, if you grow the way I grew up, you will be successful. I hope they are better than me.

My brothers and I became American citizens about three years ago. There were a lot of changes—they said, "OK, you ought to become an American citizen. That way you will have the rights and benefits you deserve here." That's the reason. As long as I am legal, I can go back and forth to Mexico with my passport.

But I feel Mexican. It is a privilege to get here to the United States, where better opportunity exists. In Mexico, we were not very, very poor, but you always want to have more and better if possible. Coming here, you can get a lot of things that help. That's what happened to me. I hope one day to go back to Mexico to retire, but I don't know. My family—we have two kids here and I don't know. Isabel says, "Well, we'll have to work it out. Maybe six months here and six months there."

I asked my kids—just to tease a little—"Do you guys want to go and live with me in Mexico?" My kids said, "No." If they go for two weeks, they are happy, but never any longer. They love it there, but not to live. Our children are both American citizens. My daughter— she understands Spanish, but cannot speak it. My son—he cannot write, but he can read and speak it. I am still thinking the Mexican way, but I have to respect my children's thinking. We are a family and we have to stay together.

Magic and Balance

by Robin Lail

The Napa Valley is a place of great magic, I think, a great place of rejuvenation. What is so magical about this place? I grew up at Inglenook. I remember as a child, we'd go off to travel—my mother, dad, and my sister and I—and we'd come home, and mom and dad would wax emotional over how beautiful it was here. I'd think, "Ehh—it's OK. There's no ocean. There's no big river. The hills are kind of short. It's not very big. And it's very boring. It's OK. But we could go back to Europe—that would be great!" Well, lo and behold, isn't it funny—as you get older, your eyes see differently. Now I drive around this valley and I see these vistas, they just stop me in my tracks—I think, "Oh, that's too amazingly beautiful."

When Francis Ford and Eleanor Coppola first bought Inglenook—and they've been there just over 20 years now—which is almost as long as I was living there—Francis invited me to come by. We were having a wonderful conversation, standing on the front porch, when he said, "I asked you over here today because I wanted to ask you a favor. Would you show me your secret places sometime?"

That was the beginning of my relationship with Francis and Eleanor. Here are two people who own this lovely piece of property—which is part of my soul—who have said, "You can come anytime you like. You're welcome to go hiking. You're always welcome here." Over the years, Francis and Eleanor have done many wonderful things for our family. Through their generosity, our daughter Erin was married at my childhood home, just as Jon and I were, with the reception following at the winery. It was one of the priceless events of our lives. And they have done many important things for the ranch, the greatest of which was to reunite the property in 1995. We share a great passion for this land, and because of this, we have a strong, unspoken bond. I feel as if we are members of a very special family.

There is a mystique in this valley. Maybe it's a leftover from the Indians. Sometimes—most of the time—I think it's about the land. But it's also about the configuration of the land. It's a small valley, and it captures the energy that's in it, and makes it ricochet back and forth—it recycles and recycles. This energy is why people come here.

That's where the fragile balance part comes. Napa Valley has become one of the places to be. For prestige. "I have a home in Aspen. I have a home in Napa Valley. I have a home in Puerto Vallarta." It's one of the places to be. So, we have a whole influx of people coming for a very different set of reasons. And when you talk about fragile—the environment is always fragile, and always, we must be so vigilant, but our environment surpasses the physical environment and it goes into the spiritual environment, and it goes into the demographic composition of the community, like the barbershop that is in St. Helena—the one remaining one—the little teeny hole in the wall, next to Guigni's store, where all the high school kids have gone to get their sandwiches for the last 50 years or so, and whoever owns the store has always been remarkably kind and supportive to those high school kids.

Our balance—how many young people can afford to buy a house in the upper valley? Not a lot. How many people who work in the retail rooms can afford to rent a house in the Napa Valley? They're middle-class people. How many blue-collar people can afford to live in the upper valley? In what conditions? What kind of housing do we have available for the people who are so important to our preservation? It's not me. I'm not out there in the vineyards. That is really hard work. I'm not even out there in the garden, breaking my back. I'm out there when I want to be, but I'm not out there day by day, making this beautiful garden. I'm not making this beautiful garden of the valley. Those are our friends that are so, so important to us. And they are our friends in the middle who operate our life—they give us our groceries and take care of our kids with fevers and do everything that enables us to do what we try to do. So I'm very concerned about our balance.

Coming to America

by Giulia Santi

My mother and father lived in a small village near the town
of Sassoferrato, Italy, Province of Ancona. There were four houses
attached—four families; I lived in one of the four houses. When people
married, they didn't go off to buy their own home. They moved in with
one of their parents. When my husband Alfredo and I were married,
we first moved in with his parents, then when my father passed away,
we moved in with my mother.

My father came over to the United States before he got married.
He went back to Italy to marry my mother, and then they came over
here. My sister was born in Italy, she was three months old when they
came here. My brothers and I were born in Pennsylvania, we were all
three born in the same house. When I was six years old my mother
got sick, and no one could find out what was wrong. My father took
her to many specialists, but no one could help her severe headaches.
Many times I saw my mother faint from the pain. The doctors said,
"We don't know what to do. Take her back to Italy. Maybe she'll feel
better." My mother didn't want to go to Italy. She said, "I'd rather die
than go back, I had a very hard time there. I had to work very hard.
Here everything is better." My father decided. We were all little.
Four kids. I was six years old. My little brother was only three years
old. My older brother was ten and my sister twelve. My father said,
"I have to go with you, how can you go to Italy by yourself?" We
would go back to Italy, it was 1920. I remember very well, we spent
two weeks on a ship named Dante Alleghieri. As soon as my mother
arrived in Italy, she was fine. She didn't even go to a doctor. My
father said, "After everything is settled down, we'll go back to the

United States." But by that time the war had begun, the passages had been closed. He couldn't come back.

In our town most of the people were sharecroppers. We owned our own house and property, we farmed enough for ourselves but we had nothing left over to sell. We had no money. We didn't have electricity or running water. After the war, things changed, both my brothers came back to the United States. One brother left home when he was sixteen years old. The other brother left in 1935 when he was eighteen. My father told me, "If I go to America, I'll take you with me, but I won't let you go alone. I have seen a lot of ladies go to the United States. They get married, and their husbands divorce them, and they have a very hard time. I don't want to see that happen to you." So I stayed in Italy.

I was married, I had my children, I didn't think I would ever leave Italy. After the war I received a letter from Washington, D.C.; it said, if you want to come to the United States this is your last chance. I though, "My gosh, I have my birth certificate. I was born there. Why is this my last chance?" The letter said, "You have six months to decide." I didn't know what to do. My husband kept telling me, "How can you go to the United States, we don't know how to speak one word of English, we don't have a job, and we don't have anything there." He didn't think we should leave. He had a job in Italy. He didn't know what he would find in the United States. We felt we were OK in Italy.

At the time, I was thirty-nine years old, I was not afraid. Maybe I was crazy, but I kept thinking, "I have to do it." One rich family in our town told me, "You better do it. Not for yourself, but for your three daughters. If your daughters, they stay here, they will marry a sharecropper and they will work day and night on a farm."

I had two brothers in Detroit, but my brothers didn't have enough money to sponsor us. My husband had a cousin in Lodi, his name was Americo Mondavi. He was Robert Mondavi's first cousin, so I wrote to Americo. He wrote back to me right away. He said, "Yes, my uncle Cesare Mondavi and Peter Crinella will sponsor your family, and my uncle will guarantee you and your husband a job." My oldest daughter, Iris, and I came to America first, she was fifteen years old. Julie and Anna were left behind with my husband and my mother. Julie was ten and Anna was eight. I thought my family would join me in a few months, but it was 14 months before my husband

and two daughters could come. Had I known the length of the wait I would have stayed in Italy. Fourteen months was a very long and painful time for our family to be separated.

Preparing to come here was very difficult for me. There were forms to fill out, and no one knew how to fill them out. I had a real hard time. There was a man in our village that helped me fill out the papers, but they came back three times. The last time they were returned to me, I went to town for help, but no one knew what to do. I was told that I should go to Rome. I took the train to Rome, and I stayed overnight with a friend. The next morning I went to the American Consulate. They said, "I'm sorry, but we can't do anything." I said, "Well, if you can't do anything, can you tell me who I can ask? Who will give me some information?" They said, "We don't know that kind of information." They gave me a business card—they gave me a name and address, so I walked over there. I found a very nice man who looked at the form and said, "You didn't answer this question on the back." The question asked if I had any diseases, if I had a history of mental illness, or if I had ever been in prison. He said, "See, you didn't answer this question." So he said, "I'll do everything. I'll send it back for you." In November of 1953 I was called for my visa and I had to leave in ten days. I came over on the Andrea Doria. This was three years before it went down. I was on the boat nine days with Iris. When we arrived, we stayed a couple of weeks with my brothers in Detroit, then we came across the United States to California. My husband's cousin was waiting for us at the Sacramento train station. He took us to his home in Lodi. He said, "You can stay a few weeks with us, then I'll take you to St. Helena." I said, "Oh, gosh, I have to go to St. Helena? Where is St. Helena? A month ago I left my home and I still don't know where I am going to live."

He said, "My cousin wants you to stay in his house in St. Helena."

I said, "Does his wife speak Italian?"

He said, "No."

I said, "I can't go. How can I go there if she doesn't speak Italian?"

He said, "You have to go. They have been waiting six months for your arrival."

So, I said, "Well, then take me there tomorrow, I don't want to wait two weeks. The next day we went to St. Helena.

I arrived in St. Helena in January. When I saw the sunshine, and how nice everything was, I thought, "What beautiful weather we are having." In our town, in January there was still snow on the ground.

I worked in Robert Mondavi's home for six years. I worked in the house and helped with the children. Robert Mondavi's children were young. Robert and his wife, Marge, were very nice to me. They had a lot of patience with me. I now think of what I had to do—poor Marge—maybe I made a lot of mistakes, but she never said a word to me. She was very nice, she was always pleased with everything I did.

I also thought, "What a beautiful home Robert Mondavi has, with running hot and cold water, electric stove, dishwasher, automatic washing machine and dryer. I thought, "My gosh—this is not my house, but I'm a millionaire!" I like Italy, but here is a better life.

When I came here, I was told if I wanted to get my citizenship back I would have to go to court. I didn't want to do that. If I went to court, I'd have to hire a lawyer. I didn't have money for that. If I went to court it might drag on for years. I wanted my family to join me in the United States, and I couldn't start their papers if I was tied up in court. I decided to wait five years, take classes, and become a naturalized citizen. I wanted my family here with me. So I went to San Francisco and started the paperwork for my husband and two daughters to come to the United States.

When my husband arrived, he started working at Charles Krug Winery. He worked there twenty years until his retirement in 1974.

I also worked as a seamstress at Roughriders in Napa. A lady from Calistoga worked there too. I paid her a dollar a day for a ride; she would pick me up at six o'clock in the morning. I had to leave for work before my husband, he didn't like that, he thought it was too much for me. He said, "You better stay home, because you don't make very much money. You only make one dollar an hour and you have to pay a dollar a day for a ride." After that, I started working at Charles Krug Winery. I worked on the bottling line for ten years until my retirement in 1977.

Coming to America

by Anna Santi True

In the beginning it was difficult for all of us. First of all, being separated from my mother for 14 months was very traumatic for me. I have very little memory of the time we were apart—I guess it was just too painful for me.

For my parents, work was the biggest hardship. They worked many hard, long hours, but socially it wasn't as difficult for them. There was a huge circle of Italians in the community who took our family in and helped us in many ways. They helped us set up our new home, took us shopping, and helped my parents join the Sons of Italy. Most importantly, they all spoke Italian, so my parents were able to socialize in their own language. For us three girls, it was more difficult, trying to fit in, going to school each day, sitting in class, and not understanding what was going on around us. It wasn't long, though, before we learned the language, made friends, and felt part of the group.

Julie and I started school on February 14th, Valentine's Day. Of course, we had never heard of Valentine's Day. We thought the party was in our honor. We came home very excited, with cards and candy. We told our new Italian friends about the wonderful welcome party we were given on our first day of school. We quickly found out that the celebration was not for us.

There were times when we would use the wrong word, wrong tense of a verb, or some other silly error. Those times were rather embarrassing for us—to hear little giggles and sometimes huge laughter from our classmates made us feel very uncomfortable. Looking back on it now, I'm sure some of the errors we made were pretty funny.

Many times Julie and I would argue about the meaning or the proper spelling of certain words.

We had no one at home to help us with our homework. It was all through trial and error. There was an Italian man that worked as ranch foreman at Charles Krug that was extremely helpful to us. He had no relatives in the United States, but was known to everyone as Uncle Pete. He took our entire family under his wing, and we loved him. He helped mom complete mountains of paperwork for dad, Julie, and me to come to the United States. We did not own a car for seven years, so he drove us many places. He was the one that encouraged us to go to school, study, and work hard to complete our education. He was a special friend and mentor. I remember showing him our report cards. He was always so proud and pleased of our accomplishments, very supportive. He showered us with many kind words of encouragement and always rewarded us with a dollar for work well done (even if it wasn't very well done).

Iris is very thankful to all the teachers at St. Helena High School, especially her English teacher, Mr. Passalaqua. She started tenth grade without speaking a word of English. Mr. Passalaqua was fluent in Italian, and he helped her with her homework every lunch hour for two and a half years. Not having all the credits to graduate from high school, Iris was allowed to take aptitude tests in all the subjects required to graduate. She passed the tests and was able to graduate with her class. Paul Alexander, the manager of the Bank of America, heard of Iris' accomplishments. He was so impressed with her that he attended the graduation ceremonies to show his support.

We had very few luxuries or material things in comparison to our American friends and neighbors, but in comparison to where we came from, we were living in great luxury. With the help of the Italian families in the community, we were able to work and make a home in this very, very special country. We were always grateful and excited to receive a hand-me-down. With mom's wonderful sewing abilities, she altered clothing to fit us. She somehow made all the items that were given to us fit our needs at the time. After a very short time, even dad learned to love the Napa Valley. Mom had a difficult time talking him into going back to Italy for a visit. The only thing we missed were our Italian friends and relatives.

We Are All Immigrants

by Liz Martini

As a boy my father-in-law, Louis M. Martini, was a dynamo. He told me that his mother said that he had too much energy for her to handle, so she sent him to the United States to be with his father. She put this 12-year-old Italian boy on a ship to America with his 19-year-old cousin who was working on the ship. She had no concept of the size of this country or the distance he would travel. When they got to New York, the cousin put the boy on a train with a salami, a loaf of bread, a bottle of wine, and $100, and sent him across the country to his father who had already immigrated to the North Beach Area in San Francisco. It was a traumatic experience for the young boy. He would never again travel in a country where he couldn't speak the language. As I said, Louis M was a dynamo, and by 1933 was making wine in the Napa Valley. He had married in 1916 and my husband Louis P was born in 1918.

By the end of World War I and with the repeal of Prohibition, there were still a lot of people who disapproved of wine, and there still are today. Wine-drinking in this country is very low compared to European countries. When World War II came, the government put all sorts of restrictions, price ceilings, and rationing on everything. The vintners figured they had some common problems so they organized and formed the Vintners Association. The vintners felt they had wines far superior to the wines being produced in the Central Valley, but when the repeal first came, a fellow from OPA (the World War II board that set prices) wanted to put price ceilings on the wines coming out of Napa Valley, but the vintners protested. "You can't compare our wines to the Central Valley," they argued. "Our wine is far superior. The quality of wine depends upon the effort and time you put into it; the quality depends on how you make your wine, and the land and climate where the grapes are gown." So when the man from the OPA asked, somewhat cynically, "How do you rate a fine wine?" Louis M's retort was, "Well, how do you rate Leonardo da Vinci?" That ended that conversation!

For years the valley was a rural farming area and we still are an agricultural community. People enjoy having a distance between houses and farms in a rural area; maybe this makes country people more cooperative. That's been my experience, country people are more cooperative than city people. Most of the people in the valley were immigrants, or their parents were. Immigrants had to help each other in the New Country. There was a built-in attitude of caring. Those early people came from small communities where they cared for each other and were dependent on each other. When Louis P's mother came here, for example, many of their neighbors came from the same small town in Italy. They just extended their home country to the New Land, or in our case to Livermore.

This intimacy of a small town still goes on here. Recently, I went to Calistoga, to my granddaughter's awards assembly. I think every child in that school got an award. That's the point I'm trying to make: In a big school you can't have the same sort of individual importance. In a small school, there's plenty to go around. And the parents were all so proud, you know how it is, they cheered and cheered. I thought to myself "This is what brings a small community together, you can personally participate in each others' lives."

Our children were born in Napa Valley and raised here. They left for college, but eventually they all came back. Today our daughter Carolyn is president of our company and our son Mike is the winemaker and vice-president. My husband said he was retiring, but of course, he never really did. He'd go down to the winery every day, but it was as much to see his children as to work.

My husband was just a happy person. If you look at the albums, in every picture of him, he has a grin. I have a wonderful picture taken the August before he died, he was smiling. Louis went to the hospital on a Sunday. They did all kinds of tests on him. On Wednesday the doctor came in and said, "I've got bad news for you. You've got cancer of the liver." We both shed a tear or two. And then he said, "I guess I'm going to know what happens before you do, Liz." He was one week in the hospital. He came home the following Sunday.

The doctor gave him some wonderful time-release morphine. For the first time in a very long time, he was without pain. He said, "I can't believe I'm going to die, I feel so good." He laughed and said, "It's a good thing they didn't introduce me to this earlier." He was good-natured right up to the end.

The last two weeks of his life, when people came to visit he always had a joke for them. He was laughing with them. He used to say, "Don't worry about death. This isn't bad at all!" He knew he was dying. He'd say, "Just don't worry about it." We had all been brought up to be so afraid of it. "There's nothing bad about it," he said, then he just quietly went off.

Both my father-in-law and my husband loved the land. We used to accuse my father-in-law of knowing every grapevine by name. He would drive his car back and forth through the rows of grapes. He absolutely loved the land. His family and descendants share in the passion for this land and the freedom you can experience out in the open. Out there it's just you and nature. Those men almost felt that life was a material thing that they hung onto, they loved it so much. They loved everything about life. They appreciated the bird in the hand. They didn't spend their time worrying about heaven, for them heaven was right there in the moment, heaven was on earth.

I could never have survived Louis's death without friends, without my community. Many of them had reached widowhood before me; so I'm not alone in what has happened. I adjust easily, always have all my life. My husband and I often talked about Edgehill, our home. He loved Edgehill, but he said, "When I die, sell it." And that's what I've done.

I'm in a new neighborhood, it is so sweet here. There's not a soul I knew before I moved here. The first day I moved in, a neighbor who knew my son came over with some flowers. The second day, they were having a block party and they invited me to it. At that party a girl came up to me—she was my daughter's age. She said, "You know, I lost my father last year up in Washington, but you remind me so much of my mother, I want you to meet her when she comes here." Then she came over and bought me a plant. People here have gone out of their way to be friends.

I feel young again, I can't believe it. Everything has changed so much, everything is so different, but I think Louis's philosophy was right, "If you do the right thing, you can be awfully happy, things work out." I guess that's faith.

Collective Independence

by Ron Birtcher

To create the agricultural preserve, just a handful of people united their friends and came to the blue-collar people and the gray-collar people and the other voters. Most voters are not owners of wineries or vineyards. But they had to vote yes in order to preserve the valley, so they had to be convinced. So people emerge out of the valley and say, "Look, we have to take care of the valley and the hillsides and all of the other things that go on here." They united to say, "Let's do it."

Not only have a lot of people come here out of choice, but they've come here very individually, and wanting to maintain their own independence. Nobody is here to try and fix anything. I didn't move here to fix anything. I moved here because I liked it here. Let's just keep what we have.

And it's interesting that everybody would unite to preserve the valley. When it's all through, then we dis-unite, and go back to being very independent again.

The only thing I can put my finger on—and it's really a massive thing—is the uniqueness of the individual and the independence of the people, collectively. How do you have a collective independence? I don't know, but that's what is happening here.

And that's a difficult lesson to give other communities. There are no rules or recipes. For reasons that were not specifically spelled out, things happened. And when you say, "Now let's write a book and tell others how to do it," I really don't know whether that works. I don't know that you can go into a community and say, "This is how to be a utopia. This is how to become the ultimate spot for people to live."

We could write little stories. But will other communities do it?
Probably not. You're telling them how to do it, but there has to be a
groundswell that starts out with two or three people that invite two
or three more to a Roundtable, and slowly the community becomes a
Roundtable. It takes that kind of commonality. You've got to find
commonality.

III
The
Sense
of
Community

A Valley Love Song

by Mary Ann McComber

My old but immaculately cared for, white-trimmed farmhouse
surrounded by a large lawn and white birch trees in early Autumn,
just as the leaves were beginning to turn color. I saw something
then I'll never forget: walking through the vineyards were
several brown-robed monks dressed like St. Francis.
Brown hoods, bare feet in sandals, ropes tied
around their waists, they prayed from huge, long,
brown rosary beads, also draped around their waists.
From the nearby hills, I heard bells ringing from the monastery
and wanted to stay there.

At harvest, the smell of coming vibrantly alive in the valley.
The harvest, beginning to take place, didn't happen out there.
It was a part of us. That feeling of belonging, of
being included in the talk down at the Post Office,
how many tons were picked, what the sugar content was.

Lee Stuart was in our small vineyard every day with

his tools to measure the sugar content of the grapes.

He waved at me in the house to come out and

began teaching me how to use a refractometer.

Belonging to a community that seemed to take

joy in me.

There was never any fear about doing it the wrong way.

Maybe there were other ways, but people didn't judge me.

Sure I had a lot to learn, but that was exhilarating.

Our first harvest was delayed due to heavy rains.

Before the pickers could get in the vineyards, the grapes rotted.

The idea that money and income could be connected to

this small garden of vines. The fact that this god-awful mess

made one of the best wines ever made at that time.

The look in the winemaker's eyes and in friends' eyes

left an almost giddy sense of anticipation.

Everything seemed to have a place in this new community:

everyone fit in, an ethic of partnership. Human beings

working in partnership with each other.

This was where I wanted my children

to grow up.

The cycle of the spirit turned as a landowner

adjacent to the monastery in Oakville turned her property into

a monastery for the revered Tibetan Buddhist teacher

the Chagdud Tulku Rinpoche, thought by many to be

the greatest spiritual teacher in the west today.

Their lovely meeting place in the hills:

Brown robed monks sat with lamas dressed in worn red and gold robes.

Bells rang from both monasteries while we prayed on beads of all colors.

The Tibetans feel a closeness to the American Indians.

Rinpoche had a deep understanding of their sacred

mysteries. I sat and took teachings on death and dying.

"How could I do this, being a Christian clergyperson?

Should I even be there?" The teacher smiled and

with a profound wave of love emanating from him, said

"I teach you spiritual truths. Truth is universal. Truth

is the same to Buddhist as it is to Christian."

He began telling stories while we sat overlooking the valley.

Stories of Tibet, of escape, stories of special places they call sacred

and stories of wisdom. There were no walls separating us. We were one,

teaching each other our chants and songs, guitars and organs,

bells and dorjes. Talented musicians from all over the valley

congregated with their violins and oboes.

Over the years, hundreds of people have come to

services held between the two monasteries.

Softly they came at sunset to light candles to

chant and sing.

When the Dali Lama accepted the Nobel Peace Prize,
he shared a vision he had for Tibet. He wanted
the world to consider making the entire country of Tibet
into a sanctuary where people could go to
be healed, to pray, to learn the ancient wisdom
undergirding all the major world religions.
This was possible, because it was
happening right then and there,
at that moment, in that place,
in my home called the
Napa Valley.

The Treasure

by Louis "Bob" Trinchero

My uncle came to Napa Valley in 1946. In January of 1947, Uncle John bought this old broken-down barn called Sutter Home. My family—mom, dad, my sister, my brother, and me—lived in New York City at the time, midtown Manhattan. My uncle kept writing to my father, "New York City is no place to raise kids. Come out to the country." He had already bought the winery, for $12,000, so dad could buy half of it for $6,000. My dad said, "Sounds interesting." He wanted a new life, so he came alone to check things out in summer, 1948.

Do you remember the first car that was produced after the Second World War? It was the Kaiser-Frazier. It was a pile of junk, made out of papier-maché. But it was brand new. My dad had been driving the same car for eight years, so he bought one and drove it across the United States. Then he wrote to my mother, "Come on out."

I was almost 13 years old, and I didn't want to come. I had to leave my friends. I gave away my sled and ice skates. I used to ice skate in Central Park every winter.

People in New York City didn't know much about California then. I knew that the capital was a place called Sacramento, and I had heard of San Francisco and Los Angeles, but that was all. When my mother went to the train depot to buy the tickets, she said, "I want to go to St. Helena, California." Well, they didn't know where St. Helena was, so they looked it up. It was close to San Francisco, but the train didn't go to San Francisco, because there was no way to get across the bay. So we got train tickets to Oakland, and then bus tickets to get us from Oakland to San Francisco. Of course, my father said, "No, I'll pick you up in Oakland."

The train ride was an adventure. It took us five days and four nights to get to Oakland. There was a long delay in Chicago and in Salt Lake City. I remember hitting the Great Plains. I'd sit for hours on the very end car, the club car, in the little observation deck. It was cold. Coming across the Great Plains, there was nothing but a sheet of snow and this ribbon of track. I remember going to dinner, then going to bed, getting up the next morning, having breakfast, and going out there again. It was exactly the same scenery. This train had been running all night. I thought, "How big *is* this country?" You really get a sense of its size when you go across it on a train.

Sutter Home Winery was just a big barn. Dirt floors. No electricity. They had just got running water. And there were waist-high weeds in front. It hadn't been operated since 1918. There was 30 years of neglect there and there was nothing in Napa Valley. No sidewalks. No delicatessens. I had just come from midtown Manhattan. I needed sidewalks; I needed a delicatessen. I thought, "Oh, my god! My old man has lost it! Where is this place?" I'd been to the country—we used to go to New Jersey and I saw a cow once, but this was ridiculous. This was the wilderness. My mother started to cry. She said, "Why didn't you tell me it was this way? We had a nice apartment in New York City." My dad was very practical. He said, "If I had told you, you wouldn't have come." It was pretty tough right then. I thought my mother might leave my father.

The only accommodations he could find was a small cabin in a summer campground located behind the El Bonita Motel. They had these little summer shacks. It was a kitchen and two bedrooms. No heat. One tap in the kitchen. That was all, for a family of five. The bathroom was in a separate building—a communal bath and shower. We arrived on December 5, 1948, and on Christmas Eve we had six inches of snow. My mother bought a little heater just to try to keep us warm. We came from an eight-room apartment in New York City! This was a real culture shock.

When we got there, there were 2,000 acres of tomatoes, and more prunes and walnuts than grapes. There were maybe 4,000 acres of grapes in the entire county. Cattle used to run between St. Helena and Calistoga. It was very rural. We prayed for something exciting to happen. We were farmers. We were happy for any change, any improvement.

Seeing the Treasure

I remember the first function I went to at Schramsberg. It was a luncheon for the vintners in 1966. The Lieutenant Governor was there. He was a friend of the Davies. Jack got up and talked about the valley. Here's a guy that, new to the valley, was very polished, very articulate, very intelligent, and he starts telling us, "Do you realize what a treasure you have here?" Treasure? What's he talking about? This was agriculture. So I had mixed feelings at first. I liked Jack, but he was the new guy here. Who was he to tell us what we should do and what we shouldn't do? Back then, you had to be here 20 years before you were considered a citizen, let alone a native.

But to preserve this valley, it took people like the Davies, who came from someplace else, who had seen other places be ruined. They realize what you have, but you don't, so they try to convince you: "Do you realize what you have here? Don't you want to save it?" And you're saying, "Save what?" All the new people who came during the 60s and 70s—they'd say, "I grew up in Long Beach, and I saw what they did to Long Beach. Do you want the same thing to happen here?" This was new thinking. We didn't know what Long Beach was like. When somebody from Orange County said, "Yeah, I remember when it was full of orange trees. . . ." I didn't know they once had orange trees in Orange County. Where can you find an orange tree now? People like the Davies came to Napa Valley and said, "It shouldn't happen here." And, after a while, you begin to think, "You know, they're right. By god, this is a pretty place." Especially when business got a little better and we got to travel. When you see other places, you realized what they were talking about.

The newcomers taught us that you have to preserve the land. Land use became the number one thing. We still had prunes and walnuts, but they were starting to die out, and vineyards were being planted, more and more. So, we said, "Let's keep it agricultural, let's preserve it." I'm not saying it was all selfless. Growers obviously thought, "Wait a minute—my land will be worth more. My crop will be worth more." Just like the winery definition ordinance requiring wines that say "Napa Valley" on them to be made of at least 75 percent Napa Valley grapes. It's nice to say it preserves the valley, but it also greatly increases the value of the land and the price of the crop, which is fine, because that stops it from being developed into homes. Let's face it, if land was only worth $1,000 an acre here, it wouldn't be in grapes. It would be in homes. That freeway would continue up the valley and we would have off-ramps, and we'd be a bedroom community for San Francisco. That's basically what we've tried to stop.

The first vintners came here for the love of the business, but we did too good a job and created a treasure. Once you create a treasure, everybody wants part of it. So, we may be defeated by our own success. Now people come and say, "$100,000 an acre? Who cares? I've got $20 million I can spend."

Success

People ask me, "What caused your success?" I can say White Zinfandel was the right wine at the right time, but the community also had something to do with it. The community set up our success. Something kept me here. Something made me do it. So, the community and the environment played a part. Who do I pay back for my success, my luck? The community. Do whatever I can to help the environment, to help the community. The team needs shirts, we need a childcare center—whatever the cause happens to be, it takes money. True, there are people with money that don't do anything with it, but for my family, we feel so fortunate, we'd like to pay back the community that made it possible.

For a while, we gave wine and money to anyone who asked. Then, 15 years ago, we decided there had to be some rhyme and reason, so my brother and sister and I sat down—we're the owners of the place—and said, "Let's put a little structure to this. Who do we want to help?" The answer was the children. That's where 85 percent of our community support goes—to the Boys and Girls Club, childcare, sports programs, schools, and libraries.

We have always had a sense of family. We had to count on each other, because things were not always good. We almost lost the winery a couple of times. We all had to work. In 1960, when my uncle retired and my father and I became partners in the winery, I just worked seven days a week. During the week, we made the wine, bottled it, and shipped it. On the weekends, we worked the tasting room. We'd bring our kids, even when they were babies, in a playpen, to the tasting room.

Family is first. It always has been. It's the most important thing to us. The winery is just the glue that keeps the family together. When you make decisions for the winery, you really are making decisions for the family. That's why my sister, my brother, and I get along very well. Because decisions aren't made for the winery, they're made for the family.

I'll get up in the morning and think, "Boy, I've got this great idea!" I come in and say, "Rog, I've got a great idea." He says, "I don't like it." So then, I try to convince him. He'll be nice and say, "I don't like it because. . . ." And we'll discuss it. Now, if we can't agree, what happens? It doesn't get done. It's as simple as that. We walk away from it, because *he* is more important to me than this winery.

Wholly communion

by Ruth Berggren

come one, come all
community

community in unity: immunity

commune with ease
immune from disease

communication: community action
compromises: community promises

community, municipality
munificent, magnificent commonality

well communities
welcome unities

Time in a Farming Community

by William Jarvis

My wife Leticia and I were attracted by the way of life that goes with an agricultural—and particularly a wine-growing—community. Our first introduction was when we were leading a very busy life down in the peninsula and San Francisco. We came up here once, and I had this idea to look at Luther Burbank's house. I'd heard that there were still some of his old fruit trees there that he had worked on. My first introduction was to Sonoma Valley, but I think the idea is kind of the same. It's a wine region. I went into the plaza there—it's a beautiful plaza.

I looked around for somebody to ask. There was a fellow sitting on the sidewalk in a wicker chair in the shade, reading the newspaper. So I went over to him and said, "Can you tell me where Luther Burbank's place is?" And he put his paper down, and rolled his glasses back, and looked up at me, and he says, "You're from out of town. You're probably from San Francisco." I said, "You nailed me. That's it." He said, "I can tell, you know. After you've been up here a while, you tend to slow down." It was such a nice way to say, "Look, you're up here in this wonderful country. Just take it easy. Take it easy." And then he proceeded to tell me where to go to find Luther Burbank's place. But I've always remembered that guy. I thought he captured the essence of the wine country. You can't be in too big a hurry.

We are very subject to nature. 1997 was a great year. 1998 was a disaster, agriculturewise, because of El Nino. So, you're very close to nature. You watch each storm, each rainfall. Last week—in April—it froze most every night. Completely unusual, but each year is unusual. Every night I listen for the wind machines to go off. They've protected us so far this spring—they've given us that extra few degrees of temperature increase to keep us from freezing. It would have never occurred to me to be so interested in the weather and the changing of the seasons. It all relates to our vines and their progress.

Last year—1997, actually—we had what we considered the year of the century for wine. The perfect year, from bud break to harvest. The weather was just perfect. Now we have to wait until the year 2002 to market this wine. That takes patience. You have to be careful of the wine during this period of time, do all the right things to bring it along. So in this agricultural world, particularly in the winery world, there is an element of long-term thinking, conservatism, guarding what we have, and not being in too big a hurry. Thinking of what this wine is going to be like four years from now, and then thinking what our vineyards are going to be producing ten years from now, or beyond my own lifetime, what is it going to be like for our children, and our grandchildren. Wine gives you a long-term perspective. You start thinking about conservation—what is this stream going to be like for my grandchildren? What is this wine going to be like for them? What are the vineyards going to be like? Are we going to keep our soil from eroding? You tend to think long term. I suppose that is the magic of this region.

Cooperative Competition

by Richards Lyon

Napans live in one of the world's largest and most visually satisfying gardens. My wife Carol and I moved to the Napa Valley in 1969. I considered the one-hour drive to my medical practice in Berkeley a small price to pay for the privilege of being part of a community blessed with a verdant land and an involved citizenry deeply concerned with preserving it. But we looked at the valley more as a garden than a working community.

When I retired from active practice fourteen years later, I found myself, with camera in hand, walking through the vineyards, intent on photographing the beauty and motion of the field workers pruning, picking, and digging, always exposing their joy with banter and song. I found myself asking winemakers and growers lots of questions. My pattern was the one that had guided me through my years in medicine. I had to understand, not memorize. The same patience and joy that the pruners and pickers displayed were equally evident when I began talking with the viticulturist and winemaker. They never seemed hurried or bored as they answered my most basic questions. Everyone had time to help me learn.

Medicine between 1940 and 1980 enjoyed 40 years of earth-shaking advances, all accomplished by practitioners and researchers working in close teamwork. Our patients were receiving the best of and latest in care because we worked together in cooperative competition. We wanted to make major strides in science and medicine, and we knew we couldn't do that by working alone. We had to share our knowledge in order to succeed.

Napa is blessed with possibly the highest concentration of educated farmers in the world. And what does their professionalism offer? The chance to develop a finer grape and a finer wine. And what are their hallmarks, visible to valley resident and visitor alike? The rows on rows of meticulously cared for vines, each vineyard seeming to have its own distinguishing marks.

A vine seems to have an individuality not seen in waves of grain. All vines are subject to diseases, such as the bacteria of Pierce's Disease, transmitted by the Sharp Shooter leafhopper, nematodes waiting to devour new growth, or the deadly louse phylloxera, always in the soil but neutralized by "resistant" root stocks. Each viticulturalist knows his plants—I suspect some know them by name—as tell-tale signs are looked for. As pruning techniques have matured, most vines are allowed to grow close to a man's height, to make the most of circulation and light. The individual vine is analyzed, to have leaves removed for better photosynthesis, and bunches of grapes are sacrificed to maximize the potential for quality.

As a physician, I am at home in this vineyard world of caretaking and individual attention to the delicate vines. As in the medical world, "Rounds" regularly take place where beginners just out of UC Davis or Fresno State meet with the wise older heads to discuss their problems, with full open sharing of experience and new ideas. Woe be it to the experienced vineyard manager who believes he has all of the answers and doesn't attend to listen to the new ideas of the smart kids coming out of graduate school. Competition? You bet. It's cooperative competition, as in the medical arena, where each viticulturalist nurtures the vines and shares knowledge with colleagues, recognizing that cooperation will result in healthier, more productive vines for everyone.

The future of the Napa Valley depends on three critical elements. The first we can take no credit for. It is the fertility of the river bottom and alluvial cover of diverse sedimentary and volcanic origin, warmed by a variety of climates that is wonderful for growing grapes. The second is the highly educated group of young winemakers and viticulturists working in intense harmony with nearby university scientists, all dedicated to producing an ever-healthier vine and finer wine. And the third element is extremely critical to the preservation of this valley. It is the community. It is the valley residents, appreciative of the special place they live in, intelligently and conscientiously trying to balance pressures for growth with sensible environmental needs. We need to recognize the substance that makes this beauty possible.

A Fair to Remember

by Ron Birtcher

Let me briefly look back a few hundred years and ask, "Where did the concept of 'Fair' come from?" It really came from people in the European countryside needing to come into the city every Friday to sell their wares. If you were a farmer growing potatoes, or if you were knitting sweaters in your little house while dad was out growing potatoes, you had to do something with them. So every Friday, you came down to the city to sell them. Basically, people would get together to show off and sell their wares.

There was an exchange of culture, too. The hill people came down and met the flatland people. The north people met the south people. One person would say, "Your family does a real cute little dance that I really like. If you show me your dance step, maybe I can play it with my little reels on my new fiddle." And suddenly a new culture began.

Fairs have always been places where new things are brought down, new ideas are shared, products are displayed, art is shown, music is played. It is a time of celebration. In America, the fair was a very important part of every single community. There wasn't a community in America that didn't have a fairgrounds. It was part of helping a child grow up in the community. Parents would say, "Billy, you are going to make your sheep better. We're going to take it to the fair in the spring, and we're going to be in the competition." Billy would be heartbroken if he didn't get a ribbon, and his mom and dad would be disappointed, but he would work harder next year. That's how the American spirit was born.

Fair in America was really part of the creation of independence and freedom. It was also a symbol of music and the arts and the crops. Hawkers came in from the manufacturing communities, and they'd tell you how to harvest fruit faster, mechanically till the soil, and sell vacuum cleaners and all the other new household aids. It was a way to introduce into the community new merchandise that wasn't yet available in the local stores. They used to sell encyclopedias there. Most of the families in America wouldn't have encyclopedias if they hadn't bought them at the fairs. Fairs really provided great change in America when television and the Walmarts weren't there. Now that the Walmarts, television, and the internet have come, and education is so fast—everything is so fast—the fairs themselves need to change.

Today, most fairs are the same old thing, with plants and flowers and animals and preserves and cakes, and hawkers from all over the country, and a Ferris wheel—just like it used to be. My wife Joanne might go down there with her jar of peaches. She wants to win a ribbon because her preserves are the best—that still goes on down there. However, if fairs just show you twenty kids and their little ducks and chickens and cows, you don't get too excited anymore.

Why are the fairs in California failing? Because nobody ever challenged them to do anything different, and they were only used for about five days out of the year, and the rest of the time the ground sat idle. That's crazy.

The Napa Fair was given an opportunity to reinvent itself so that it would communicate with the community of tomorrow. We're separating ourselves from the California State Fair system, and we're forming a brand new nonprofit organization in which we are reinventing our relationship to the community and its current changing needs. Most fairs and fair boards ask, "Why aren't we making money like we used to in the 40s? Whatever happened to the 60s when we used to do it this way, or that way?"

Our fair is determining where it fits in the Napa Valley of tomorrow. We have to change it to meet the times and conditions over the next couple of decades. And that's what we're in the process of doing. Part of the fair process is what built the American process.

As America changes, the fair has to change—to use the whole fair-grounds more efficiently and effectively and still serve the community. But serve it every day, every week, every month.

The fair is what community is all about: people coming together, doing things, bringing things, exchanging, expanding, and growing. Bringing and taking; and talking and sharing; and crying and dancing. All of those things happen at the fair.

Hospitality and Community

by Jamie Davies

Our sense of community and hospitality in the Napa Valley remains as strong today as it was when we first moved to the area in 1965. While over time there has been a dramatic change in how things get done day-to-day, the spirit and dedication that inspires those activities remains the same.

In the 1960s, we entertained our neighbors at home and they returned the hospitality, it was usually potluck. We all took great satisfaction in those gatherings. They were relaxed; you could bring the family.

We entertained at home because it was a natural thing to do. We didn't have much in the way of restaurants, theater, art, music, or cultural activities. A two-hour trip to San Francisco was required for that. Among winery, community, and family responsibilities, those trips were rare.

Family celebrations were frequent and shared with others. These continue and have become more frequent with our expanding circle of good friends. This is something we will never lose. There are many more entertainment options in the valley today. Still the Schram barn and our mountain vineyard picnic grove remain favorite sites for my family to gather.

From the beginning as winery owners, we entertained a wide range of guests from near and far, who were accustomed to the finest cuisine. As we were producing what we considered to be exemplary sparkling wines, we wanted to enjoy them in the company of good food. Up to a point we did all the preparations ourselves. But as it is wont to do, life evolved to the point where our other responsibilities made it impossible to do all the work ourselves. We wore too many hats, and there were too many guests to entertain.

I still feel that the simple approach to entertaining is what our guests appreciate most. We should be more in tune with the land and the seasons, using the products that are grown nearby as opposed to ordering things that are shipped great distances. Communing in nature with a bottle of champagne, fresh food, and good friends is what we do best.

In the early 70s I joined with a group of local women to create the Napa Valley Cooking School as a way to improve our culinary skills. We formed a steering committee to direct the school programs. We invited professional chefs to demonstrate cooking techniques to the vintners' wives and other women who liked to cook. Sally Schmitt's Chutney Kitchen at Vintage 1870 in Yountville was the school's first home. Eventually it moved to Trefethen Winery.

The first year the chefs were not professionals. Like myself, they were good home cooks. Participants in these classes would make suggestions for the next session. We called on friends, or even friends of friends, from Berkeley or San Francisco, who had some unique talents to share with us. Every year we came up with a new group of instructors for the six weeks of one-day sessions. Eventually we lined up chefs from outside the Bay Area from cities like Los Angeles and Chicago. With the growing demand we expanded the program. The chef would prepare the same menu two days in a row because we had so many people who wanted to be part of the school. We held classes in the winter months because that was the so-called slow time in the wine business. If there ever is, or was, a "slow" time.

The chefs loved it because they were drawn into our community of vintners' families and friends. Many of them had never been here. We put them up for the night in our homes; one of us would host them for dinner, invite a few locals, and give them a little flavor of the Napa Valley. Thus we began interacting with the chefs of America who were representing our wines in their restaurants, but who were also on the cutting edge of American cuisine. Chefs contributed their time, charging only for their travel and lodging expenses. All of the money we collected in class fees was donated to Napa County charities.

We learned a lot from each other. There was a real synergy in these classes. We learned from the chefs and, in turn, shared the valley experience with them. Lasting friendships developed as we became increasingly involved with entertaining, the culinary arts, and the pleasures of pairing fine wines with a range of food preparations. The chefs were interested in the finest ingredients. Before they planned their menus, they would go to Napa and Sonoma to meet the specialty farmstead growers and see what produce was available. Because we knew the farmers, we could plan an itinerary and accompany them on these visits. This convened chefs, farmers, and vintners to celebrate the best of cooking. Through these shared experiences we came to understand the balance that exists between the earth and those who enjoy its bounty. If you give a little you get so much in return. Through this exchange, we become members of the community.

A lot of things have evolved simultaneously as a result of people really caring for one another and for the land, working with each other for mutual benefit. I don't think I've ever been in a place where there was so much activity designed to help build a better community.

When my husband Jack became ill, Lila Jaeger organized my women friends to create a food bank for us in order to free me to take care of him. We had a sort of "Meals on Wheels." Every couple of days somebody arrived at the back door. They were asked not to come in the front door for fear of disturbing us. They would enter by the kitchen entrance, leave their food on the table, and disappear. These dear friends really knocked themselves out. Complete meals just showed up, wonderful, delicious, and ready to eat.

When Jack passed away, word got around about the date and time of the memorial service in our vineyards. I was stunned at the wave of responses from the restaurants, hotels, resorts, the Culinary Institute of America, and the people who supply rentals and other services—these special neighbors just appeared bearing gifts. They brought food, servers, carvers, chairs, free printed materials, whatever they could offer. Members of the community really wanted to do something. They wanted to say, "Thank you." Or, "I respect what you did for Napa." And many wanted to get up and talk. They really had a lot to say, which wasn't just about Jack, but about how they viewed the Napa community. It's all tied together. It was very moving. That ceremony was much too long—we had to bring the eulogies to an end as the sun was sinking over the horizon. People were very still. A good percentage of them were standing because we didn't expect nearly that many people to come. It was amazing. Totally amazing. For me, this outpouring of love and kinship from the

community really cemented my trust in the harmony that exists
between the land and its people.

As individuals we all feel insignificant and humble when we arrive
at a new place. But we have energy, enthusiasm, and anticipation for
discoveries we will make. We respect others in the community. We
know we don't have the right to come and force our ideas on people.
It is important to listen and to ask, "What are you really trying to
achieve here and how can we work together to make it happen?"

This same spirit influences our families as well. They are naturally
connected with this positive energy. Our children are at a pivotal
point in their lives right now as they are finding their own place in
this complex world. They have developed respect and pride in our
heritage. They believe in it. Although they want to identify with it,
they don't know how to respond to it. Some have figured it out. The
important thing is that this life continues from one generation to the
next, that we all learn from one another as we move forward.

To build community, you have to get involved. There is no substitute for involvement. You have to start with something that resonates
with you; somewhere you think you can make a difference. You must
be true to your own vision and voice. It will eventually lead you to
where you ought to be. In the course of your involvement you learn
and grow, getting more in return than you might expect. This is what
life is all about. There is the power in each of us to transform our
world. If we work together, we have the ability to accomplish so much.
We can each improve the quality of life in this place we call home.

Women and Community

by Robin Lail

The people who built the first wine auction were my women friends. You may find one or two in a community—or maybe four or five of them—but in a community this size, to have such a concentration of creative, energetic, buoyant, positive, enthusiastic, can-do women is really amazing.

The women of Napa Valley are remarkable. Their attributes are legion and include intelligence, generosity, nurturing attitudes, creativity, hospitality, vision, and humor. Since we are all extremely busy, there may be great gaps of time between visits, but should something go wrong in someone's family, the women lock arms and rally, bringing an incredible buoyancy to an otherwise unhappy turn of events.

What kinds of things am I talking about? A vintner became extremely ill and one woman set about making a network of meal providers. Each person was to bring an evening meal in disposable containers and place it quietly in the kitchen each afternoon. Since there were some 40 women participating in this outreach, no one ever felt any burden, only joy at being able to help friends in some small way. Another group of women have spent considerable time researching the possibility of establishing a "safe house" for friends when the onslaught of old age makes it impossible to fend for yourself.

And then there are the remarkable individual contributions— Mary Ann McGuire has become a prominent feature in many celebrations of life, illness, and death. She is treasured for her gift of hope and her enthusiasm for all of life and what goes beyond. Molly Chappellet has given the gift of beauty, not just to her community but to the world at large. Belle Rhodes has contributed enormously to the world of good taste through her cooking classes and her intense involvement in the world of food and wine. Margrit Biever Mondavi has contributed so much to the success of the Robert Mondavi Winery as she has woven consumers into the mix and made them friends through her summer concerts, art shows, and cooking schools. She has created the most amazing role model for hospitality that I can imagine, which is so vertical in its nature that it doesn't matter who walks in the door. They're equally warmly received.

Our women are very active, charitably and quietly. There is an enormous amount of giving which occurs behind the scenes—giving of time, energy, vision, and funds.

Everybody has stories that are so precious and so moving and so life-changing. That story is a part of the whole story—our story. It's just a part of our struggles as human beings to do all these things that we try to do—to be decent and to be noble and to be caring and good. And there are amazing obstacles that come in the way, which is what makes you appreciate this wonderful sense that you have these friends around. If you get into deep doo-doo, they're just there. You can turn around and say, "Help!" That knowledge is so reassuring in your heart.

IV
The
Spirit
of
the
Valley

Indian Story

by Mary Ann McComber

While the children were still small, we began building a new home on a ranch a few miles from the farmhouse where all the children had been born. We discovered that part of the ranch had been Indian burial grounds. People and neighbors living on this land were deeply connected to the memories of the Indians. Our dentist had grown up here and, like his sons, he walked the valley year in and year out, fishing or searching for arrowheads. The obsidian would sparkle like black mirrors after a rain, and if you were lucky you found beads. We found treasures of them on the ranch. We were haunted by the presence the Indians left behind. It took no stretch of the imagination to see where and how these people lived.

For four thousand years, before the oldest living redwood tree began pushing its way up through the earth's crust, the Wappo Indians lived, worked, and played here in harmony with the environment, caring for its bounty and settling any rivalries with their Pomo and Miwok neighbors in a short, timely manner. They never imagined that life as they knew it could come to an end. However, in 25 years, between 1836 and 1861, they were completely displaced from their ancestral homes. George Yount, an early Napa Valley pioneer, estimated that 8,000 Native Americans lived in the Napa Valley, but by 1850 he reported that less than 500 remained. By 1908 only 40 Wappo could be found anywhere.

In 1823 Father Altimira, the Franciscan priest who first explored the Napa Valley, found people living here peacefully in pole houses, using clamshell beads and magnesite cylinders for money and jewelry. They feasted on the plenitude of Napa Valley's grains and plants supplemented by seafood and the abundant freshwater shellfish and salmon found in the Napa River. Acorns, rich in protein, carbohydrates, and fiber were the staff of their diet and their favored foods. Dried seaweed and salt, gathered during annual treks to the Sonoma County coast, were cached with thankfulness and reverence, since plants as well as animals were considered sacred. Fowl and game completed their diet.

Biologists tell us that this sacred valley was lovingly tended and managed, but without tools or methods the European is familiar with. The Californian Indians, Wappos included, approached resource management from a different perspective than we do. We tend to think in terms of "level it or leave it natural." The Californian Indian thought "care for it and gather sustenance from its bounty." Unable to understand the ways of the early California Indian, American settlers gave them the derogatory name "digger Indians," suggesting they were hunter-gatherers who aimlessly and haphazardly managed to extract meager sustenance from the earth. As it turns out, nothing could be further from the truth.

California's indigenous people utilized a millenia-old wisdom of wildlife conservation and resource management that kept California's hills and plains the Garden of Eden reported by her early explorers. For the Wappo and other California tribes, the plant world is a sacred one, central to their culture. The Wappo method of resource management guaranteed the healthy, bountiful harvests they needed for food, medicine, ceremonial plants, and the materials to make their baskets—for which they were famous. They gathered only what they needed and they took care of what they had. For example, when they gathered seed for pinole (a native cereal), every few handfuls they would cast some back to the ground to assure a bountiful harvest the following season. When they gathered corms, bulbs, and tubers, such as wild onion and Indian potatoes, they deliberately aerated the soil with their sharpened digging sticks, creating a friable growing medium that would yield large crops the next year. Any smaller, dormant bulbs found attached to the parent were removed and replanted. The constant aeration of the soil as people gathered food and basketmaking material not only prevented disease but encouraged the root growth necessary for increased plant vigor, while stimulating the kind of growth necessary for premium basketmaking materials.

Coppicing and burning were two other techniques used exten-
sively throughout California. To coppice a shrub is to cut it almost
to the ground. Although it may seem a destructive act, in reality the
practice encourages the plant to flourish and stimulates the growth of
the long, straight, slender branches so highly prized for basket and
tool making.

Kroeber and Heizer wrote: "The Indians' preservation of the
land and its products for the 10,000 years or more of their undisputed
occupancy was such that the white man wrested from them a garden,
not the wilderness it salved their conscience to call it."

In 1835, George C. Yount was riding his horse "Hunter" along
a narrow, winding trail on Mt. St. Helena when his eyes grew wide
with wonder, for he spied a spot of more earthly beauty than he had
ever seen or heard of before, a valley covered with rank wild grasses,
interspersed with blue and gold patches—the blue of lupin, the gold
of poppy—and dotted with clumps of live oak, laurel, and madrona.
Buckeye, ash, and manzanita held sway. Willows, alders, and wild
grapes bordered the stream. Pine, redwood, and fir crept up the sides
of hills carpeted with alfilaria, pin grass, and burr clover, bathed in
the rays of the setting sun and tinted with purple shadows in their
depths.

He smelled the fragrant lilac. He heard the song of the lark, the
call of the quail, and the plaintive note of the dove. And he felt that
somewhere he had known it all before. In the hush of the late afternoon, as the valley lay painted in a glory not of this world, his lips
whispered the prayer: "In such a spot I would clear a bit of ground
and build a home; in such a spot I would live and die."

A Small Town Church

by Steve Lundin

I wanted to move to a small town and a small church. St. Helena and Napa Valley were not on my mind particularly at all. When I got a call from my superintendent saying, "We want to appoint you to the church in St. Helena," it didn't immediately click where that was, even though I had grown up in northern California. Before the appointment was finalized, my wife and I took a trip to the Napa Valley. We were driving down 29. It was rainy, but just as we were entering the valley, there was a rainbow and the sun was coming up. We both gasped and said, "Here I am, Lord! Send me!"

Coming from an urban area, we felt immediately that life is more whole and integrated. Life is more holistic. The boundaries between church and community are much fuzzier in a small town. You relate to the same people in City Hall that may be in your pews on Sunday.

The church is right across the street from where my kids are in school. They were popping in to the office to check in after school. If one of them was in trouble, I was popping in over there. We live close to the church, so they could be on foot or on bike much easier here than when we were in Sacramento. So the family kinds of things were immediately delightful for us. It didn't take me long to realize that it's a pretty special community, and to feel pretty well integrated into it. I think that when you come to a place with kids, that really helps.

One of the things I've noticed with members of the congregation who are fairly new and around my age is that they come searching for a small town church. They're searching for this kind of life—where you go to the park after church and have lunch together with other families. There's a real hunger for that.

The sanctuary itself is from 1869. It has that wonderful country church feel to it. People walk into it and fall in love with the space. Soon after I arrived, we received some donations and were able to restore it in a way that had real integrity with the way it was built. For instance, it has these wonderful pressed tin ceilings. The room next to it, even the walls are pressed tin. It's just gorgeous. We were able to patch that and repaint it and put new carpet and new pews in, but it has that charm of a small town church that was built a century ago. One of the things that I've noticed is that people or visitors who don't really have a relationship with God or who are searching for God, but haven't been connected with an institution, come to this church, this place of prayer, and sigh—as if they've found a home. They feel very connected to this place.

McCormick Ranch

by Babe Learned

My great-grandparents came to California with the Gribsby Ide party. My grandmother, Molly, was the first baby born under the Bear Flag in Sonoma and was known all her life as The Bear Flag Baby. As a wedding gift, Molly and her husband received the McCormick Ranch, which was about 3,000 acres.

My father lived at the ranch all his life of 92 years. I always remember him being on a horse. My dad would drive his cattle down Spring Mountain Road. Miss Dickinson, who used to live on Spring Mountain Road, would say Hail Marys—"Here comes John McCormick with all his cattle. Spread out, you fellas, and duck under a tree!" She used to say that every year!

When I graduated from high school, I left. I couldn't wait to get out of here. I got married and moved back east. When my husband was overseas in World War II, I came back home to the ranch.

We had 3,000 acres: 1,500 acres in Sonoma County and 1,500 in Napa County. At one spot, on the top of a mountain, we have a 360-degree view, where my husband watched the Bank of America being built in San Francisco. He'd ride his horse up there and he'd watch it all. We used to go there when we were kids. We'd ride our horses on moonlit nights and watch all the lights in San Francisco. And in September, the sunsets on the ocean—I've never seen anything—in Hawaii, Europe, or anyplace—that equals that. Fantastic. It happens only about ten times a year. It lights up the whole ranch and then it sets. We would watch the sunset sink into the ocean. At one time we watched Sputnik go by. It was in the paper the next day.

My daughter Sandy didn't have much to do with the ranch, until she had her children. And now she absolutely loves it. In my day it wasn't worth what it is today. So she couldn't afford to inherit it when I passed away. She decided that she would like to do something with the property to preserve it from generation to generation. We created the McCormick Sanctuary. We partially gave and partially sold 1,000 acres to be a part of Sugarloaf Ridge State Park. My daughter has done a great thing with this land. Hundreds of children and teachers now visit the sanctuary each year.

I think we have 750 acres left. I've got some in the grandchildren's names and I've kept some. I have a favorite place down at the creek. It's just wonderful. So I kept about ten acres there for picnics and so on.

In the summertime, I used to take my horse out and I would say, "Gee. There's just God up there. And I'm out here alone." I have a hard time going to church. Because it's all there on the ranch. It's there with you. I'd be alone. And I would be thinking, even as a kid, "You know, there's just God and me out here."

Today I am 83 years old and, you know, I feel the same way about this land as I did when I was a kid. It's about me and God and, now, all the children who come to visit.

A Collection of Thoughts about Napa

Geopolitical

Napa County is geopolitical. The political and geographic boundaries are the same. We're surrounded essentially by a mountain range—
or hills. It makes it very simple. We're only thirty miles long and five
miles wide, or whatever, so we do know each other. Look at the fair
in Napa. It's one of a handful of fairs in the state that's profitable.
Most of the fairgrounds in the state lose money. When you go to the
fair, everybody's there. It's a party. It's gotten so that they have a
party the night before the fair, just to have a party for people to go to.
It's a fun get together. There are no rides or anything. You just have
a glass of wine and hors d'oeuvres and see each other, before the kids
get there.

That gives us a common identity. A common edge. We're not
spilling out into a variety of other areas. I think that's a major factor.
Because you can get to people. It's not that we all think alike. We've
got a lot of diversity in this community. But it helps us. We have
to work together. We recognize that. It helped with Measure A and
other issues.

—Brian Kelly

Diversified communities

Banks are measured by our involvement in the community. The
way the government comes in and monitors us is to look at the census
tracts. Where is the poor census tract? There are 20–22 census tracts
in the county. There is no census tract that is more than 2 to 2.5 of any
other census tract in almost any indicator you could pick—income,
housing costs, rentals, etc. These are large-area census tracts. And the
big houses are next to small houses. But if you average the census

tracts in Napa, there's no poor area. The lowest one is about one-half the average rental, the average housing cost, the average income of the other areas. That may be significant. People are mixed throughout the community. Now, there are housing issues. It's not to say we're clean. What I perceive to be a major issue in the valley is affordable housing.

In a lot of communities, housing stock gets much more regimented. You have suburban areas that are much more consistent. In Napa, people aren't winding up in these consistent enclaves, whether they're very poor or very rich or whatever. They're seeing a more diversified world.

—Brian Kelly

American Center

I'm involved in the American Center for Wine, Food, and the Arts. It was a dream of Robert Mondavi's for years to have a cultural center, and they put a board together and have raised dollars. A number of people put $10,000 in to start. That's the founding 70 group. To be on their board, you had to give substantially more than that. My advice is: Form an advisory board that is the fabric of your neighborhood. Use that group as ambassadors to help sell the American Center to the community of the Napa Valley. These people will cover for you when you have to go before the City Council.

—Brian Kelly

In the nonprofit world in the county of Napa, there's tremendous repetition. They all want their own building. They don't all need their own building. They all want their own computer systems and executive directors. They could share a lot more. They have lots of the same people on their boards. They could consolidate some of that time and money.

—Brian Kelly

Family community

There's an issue that's interesting about this community. Napa is what I would call a "spousal" community. I've worked in the Bay Area—all over the Bay Area—San Francisco, Oakland, Berkeley, Marin, San Jose, and here. Napa is the only community that I've worked in where events are spousal——you are expected to bring your spouse with you. I remember a dinner party for our board of directors. One board member just understood that spouses were coming to dinner. It was a Friday night. Your spouse comes with you. The host, who was from New York, didn't understand this. He rapidly learned! When you go to events for fundraisers or work, it's for couples.

Where do children fit into this? It's not just that my wife goes with me; so do my children. Our kids always went with us. Are the children as involved in other communities? It flabbergasts me, how involved these children are. I think that's why there aren't more kid problems in Napa. These kids are buried in things to do. Leadership, volunteering, sports. Where do the children fit in? Maybe that's part of the solution. Continue to work with the schools. It will make for an interesting community to see how the children come through this whole process. If the children are in the fabric of the community, what are they going to be like?

—Brian Kelly

I have rarely found gender to be an issue in the Napa community. One memory I have makes the point very well. In the late 60s or early 70s, Superior Court Judge William Blankenburg called us to say that we had been selected to serve on the Napa County Grand Jury. In those years, the two Supreme Court judges proposed the names for the Grand Jury. He told us to talk it over and decide which of us would serve. We decided that Jack had more time in the evenings, when the meetings were scheduled, so he served, but the choice was ours to make. Either one of us could have gone.

—Jamie Davies

Growing up

Everyone knew you. They knew where you came from. They knew what was going on in your life. They knew how to comment or treat you. If something was going poorly, they were able to take care of you. If something was going well, they were able to cheer you on. The community was really tight. I didn't realize it until I left . . . when I went into a bigger pond.

—Aimee Price

Design

The base of my design is the oak tree. The solidness of it. The beauty of it. How it works so well with its environment and its surroundings. If one thing goes wrong, it dies. Too much water—it goes. Too much pollution, too many beetles—it's not a durable tree. That's the way I'd like to see development happen. Work with the land. Work with your environment. Don't work against it. You see it happening all the time. You see developments that don't work, that are counterproductive. Growing up in the Napa Valley has had a huge impact on how I do my work as a designer. Just look at how nature works with itself here. Look at a meadow or the spring flowers. That's a palate that can be used in almost any interior. The mustard and the grass and the browns in the hills and the blues in the sky. They change every season. The colors in the hills change with the blue, and that's a shade you can work with. Nothing in particular stands out. Everything works together. Your eye is never drawn to one thing. It's drawn to the whole.

—Aimee Price

Hospitality

I grew up in New Orleans, where hospitality and graciousness is of primary importance. As a child, you're trained in that, socially and environmentally. Much of the grace in New Orleans comes from the way the houses are built, and the way people treat each other, and the trees. The trees and the flowers. I have that same feeling of graciousness and of grace, but here in Napa I feel it more in relationship to the earth and how the sky touches the mountains. How you move along through the mountain ranges and you come across this valley and that valley and this corner of a valley. I feel a lot of grace. I feel invited in. There are some very beautiful places on the earth that have a more foreboding grace—more distance. But here there is a hospitality and graciousness. I feel very invited in, graciously welcome.

—Rosemary Partridge

Environment

People are becoming more conscious of our environment all over. Even government—state and federal government—is becoming more involved. The people who move here come here because it is a wonderful place to live, and the reason it is that way is because we have been able to preserve the open area. We are learning what makes a healthy stream, we'll bring the river back better than what it is now.

—Tony Holzhauer

The Ag Preserve

The future of the Napa Valley and the Agricultural Preserve is dependent on three factors: (1) a Board of Supervisors willing to support it; (2) a body politic willing to elect that Board of Supervisors that commits to it; and (3) an industry that can pay the bills. If you take away the economic structure and the wine industry doesn't function any more, then these fellows who have all this investment in land are going to be very anxious to do something else with it, and there will be a tremendous amount of pressure to create alternatives to this economic decline. But you can chip away at the Ag Preserve. It will be one of those things where you look out one day and say, "What happened?" I tell people that the real land-use issues are fought one foot at a time. The big issues are always going to die. People aren't going to vote for massive change. But we can chip away, and that's the real threat.

—Mel Varrelman

You can actually look out onto a lake from a balcony and find it to be clear one day and filled with algae the next. It's not a very savory metaphor, but I'm afraid that's what's happening in this community. Everybody's pretty comfortable. It looks great. Sure, there's a house here, and an erosion problem there. But in general things look pretty darn good. People are saying, "What are all these people fighting about? It looks a lot better than Walnut Creek."

—Jeff Redding

The Spirit of the Napa Valley

by Brother Timothy

I entered Christian Brothers as a kid in 1928, just out of high school. I was 17$\frac{1}{2}$ years old. I didn't know that the Brothers had a winery, before I entered the Order. The business was small and Prohibition was on. My parents were living in the little tiny village of Cucamonga. That's been a joke on radio and TV—on the Jack Benny show—to get on the train to go to Azusa, Etiwanda, Cucamonga, San Bernardino.

I didn't know much about wine, although I lived in southern California, out in grape country, but the grapes were shipped away in 25-lb. lugboxes to people who made their own wine at home. During Prohibition, it was legal to make wine at home and drink it at home. It was illegal to carry it across the street—that's transportation. And it was illegal to sell it. But you could make it in your home or your backyard and drink it on your own property.

I started teaching chemistry in high school before I was 21. I had no questions on my mind about leaving teaching, but maybe I was struggling a bit in some classes, like religion. Repeal took place in December of 1933. In 1935, one of the Superiors came to me and asked me if I would like to go to the winery and work as a wine chemist. Since I knew some inorganic chemistry—the kind of chemistry taught in high school—it was thought that I could learn wine chemistry. It was a learning project for me, so I moved to the winery July 1, 1935.

We were so shorthanded and so desperate for money. Prohibition and the Depression overlapped each other there for a few years, and the overlap period was a pretty severe kind of depression, especially for wineries. So, it was on-the-job wine study for me while I worked at the winery. I worked in the laboratory a few hours a day and worked at other jobs other hours of the day. I've done just about every job there was to do around the winery.

In the wine business, everything is different all the time. Every year is different. Every vineyard is different. Every grape variety is different. Every wine is different. Every time you make a new wine, it's going to be a little different than anything else you have ever made before. You can't duplicate something that you made in the past, but you can work at it. You can come close.

I believe that the spirit of the Napa Valley has been a welcoming spirit, a hospitable spirit. "Open House"—tourism and tastings at wineries—started a long time ago. Hospitality is part of the fame of the Napa Valley.

The Napa Valley Vintners Association (NVVA) is a self-help organization. It's important to the Napa Valley. It started in 1943 when four people started to meet once a month to have lunch. In the very first years of the NVVA, they didn't want to make big claims, or say, "We are important people running this thing." They wanted to do things quietly and without exposure. They used to say to each other, "Oh, we're just an eating and drinking club. We meet once a month to eat and drink." Louis M. Martini was one of the leaders of the group. John Daniel of Inglenook and Louis Stralla, who later became mayor of St. Helena, and Charlie Forni. They were the first four members. They used to eat lunch at the soda fountain in St. Helena, called the Sweet Shoppe. They ate and drank there—no wine at all, just milkshakes and stuff like that. But then they graduated from that and moved over to the Miramonte Hotel and began to serve wine with their meals. It started with those four people and has grown to about 150 today.

Even when they called themselves an eating and drinking club, there was still some altruism, and the aspect of entertaining and hospitality—Open House—existed. Beringer was one of the first wineries to have the open-door policy, with visitors getting a tour of the winery and getting a few free samples of wine. The man behind that—call it a PR push if you wish—was Fred Aberzini. I think Fred didn't even taste wine, but he was a winemaker. He would invite Hollywood stars, like Clark Gable and Carol Lombard, and a lot of those old movie stars, to come to the Napa Valley and visit the winery. He would show them around and pour wine for them and give them a couple of bottles to carry away. He kept big scrapbooks of every press release and public relations thing that appeared in the papers. That was very shortly after the Repeal—before 1940.

I want to mention a very recent project here. Brother Armando Garcia, one of our Brothers, has opened up a little institute for adult education of Latinos. His place is in a little shopping mall where the old county health services was, on Old Sonoma Road. He has rented a facility, just a little place. It will hold about 35-40 people in folding chairs. That's like a classroom. He's going to do adult education there. When he rented the space, our De LaSalle Institute sent workers from here to help clean it up and fix it up and paint it up, and put some carpet on the floor, and buy some chairs and put them in. Now it's on a shoestring budget. He's not charging any tuition for anybody. He's going to depend on charity, whatever help he can get from people in the community. These are things that show you what the spirit of the Napa Valley is all about. It's self-help and volunteerism.

The volunteer spirit is also behind the Napa Valley Wine Auction— there are more than 1,000 volunteers. That's part of the spirit of the Napa Valley. Clinic Ole itself was founded to fill a need, and founded on a shoestring. It's health care for the poor people, the working people, anybody who is poor. So, Clinic Ole is very charitable, and self-help, and nonprofit. The first few contributions made by the wine auction to the Clinic Ole amounted to almost the total annual budget of Clinic Ole.

Another important issue in the valley is affordable housing. Monsigneur Brenkle, the pastor in St. Helena, has been the spearhead for that. He's been working hard at it for 10 years or more now.

The hospital volunteers work in places like the Queen of the Valley Hospital, and the Seventh Day Adventist Hospital in St. Helena has volunteers too. Volunteers are a real bedrock for the spirit of the Napa Valley. People are willing to devote time and energy and talent without pay.

A group of women—I think it was almost all women—in Napa founded a thing called Community Projects. It has been very successful over the years. It's a self-help effort, not leaning on the government or the taxpayer, but a self-help benefit thing. They've contributed a lot of money to the hospital and a couple different schools, and to other charitable, worthwhile causes.

People like Bob Mondavi deserve a lot of credit for promoting the spirit of the Napa Valley. He's putting money into the American Center for Wine, Food, and the Arts. Bob was also the number-one spearhead to get the wine auction started. And also the Center for Wine, Food, and the Arts. The Opera House restoration is another self-help thing. His wife Margrit is involved in the Opera House—it's all culture. Bob is very conscious of what he's doing. He's a very smart guy who has thought things out. And he works very hard at developing these thoughts, the programs. He's not only full of the concepts, but he's also full of generosity in support of those concepts.

The Napa Valley is showing more attempts to stick together, to work together as a unit, in a cooperative spirit. For instance, look at the vote of the taxpayers for the flood control project. This was quite an unusual thing. One or two votes had been taken before and were unsuccessful, but this last vote went through with more than two-thirds of the vote. The vote for the flood control project—a lot of people voted in opposition to their own self-interest. They were somewhat altruistic in that vote. It's good for the valley. It's good for everybody. "And if it's good for one part of the valley, then maybe, eventually, it will be good for me, but I can't see how it will be good for me right now." That shows a lot of community spirit, the spirit of the Napa Valley.

Rafael Olguin and Mary Novak

by Father Brenkle

I came to the parish in St. Helena in November, the Sunday after
Thanksgiving, so that we were into the Christmas season before I got
to know anybody. I was invited out for Christmas Eve dinner by a
family in the parish, the Olguins. I said, "Fine. I'd love that." They
live down in Lugo Park, which is a self-help housing development.

Rafael Olguin is a garbage collector for Napa. Josefina stays
at home. Both parents struggle with English. Josefina speaks very
little English. They have seven kids, who went to college at MIT, Cal
Berkeley, UCLA. . . . It's just amazing. And the children all attribute
it to their mother. In Mexico, she sent them to a neighboring school
because it was a better school. But they had to ford a river to get to
that school. The kids would take their clothes off and be in their shorts.
They'd hold their books above their heads and cross the river. Josefina
would stand there on the shore and pray. I asked her once, "Could
you swim, Josefina, if they got pulled in?" She answered, "No."
But she prayed them across.

In the meantime, I ran into Mary Novak. She also invited me
for dinner on Christmas Eve. I said, "Well, how about if I join you
for dessert? Where do you live?" She said, "At Spottswoode." I said,
"OK. I'll find it." So I went down to the Olguins, and had a very
humble but a very nice meal. The kids were wonderful. I just had a
shirt and sweater on. So then I drove to Spottswoode, and I drove
into this big circular driveway among the Jaguars and Mercedes, and
I looked into this big picture window and saw that everybody was
dressed up! I said, "Oh, what the hell! I'll go in." So I crashed the
party, and was warmly received and had a wonderful dessert there.

I drove away saying to myself, "This is an interesting place! This is going to be a challenge, with people who are worlds apart." And do you know what was beautiful, then? Midnight mass. I said midnight mass. I looked out at the congregation. There was one pew filled with all the Olguins and their very traditional dress. And then the Novaks were in a pew about three rows behind them. It was great. That, to me, has been one of the joys of this place: bringing the people of means together with the people who need means.

You have to tap in to what makes the other person tick. You have to sit down one-on-one with people. Ask them, "What excites you?" Start listening to them. What excites them might be totally different. But can you find some common ground? I come at it from a scriptural point of view, and he comes at it from an economic or work point of view. Who cares? Let's work together. And we both get what we're looking for out of this thing.

Christ was the best psychologist/social worker that you ever wanted to meet. He knew how to get people to respond. He treated people respectfully. When you just use people, then it falls apart. People get angry and resentful. When there's respect between people, good things happen. We need to respect each other.

V
The
Art
of
Community

The Jarvis Conservatory: Creating Community Through Art and Art Through Community

by William Jarvis

I have a love of education. It sounds kind of banal when you say it that way, but I spent 14 years in college. I was raised in a poor area in Oklahoma. We had very poor schools. In fact, my high school disintegrated altogether. I was able to get into the University of Oklahoma early, and that was such a great pleasure that I've been studying ever since, through formal education or otherwise. Most people can get through college in four years, but I spent 14 years going to different kinds of colleges in different countries of the world, studying different things, technical, liberal arts, languages, literature. My wife Leticia and I spent a whole year in France just studying French literature, and almost another year in Spain studying Spanish literature.

When I was a boy in Oklahoma, my father and a few other people had the idea of starting a junior college. I thought, "Why? The high school is falling to pieces. Why would you want to start a college?" They went ahead and started it. Not too long ago, I went back to my hometown, and the little junior college they started has become part of Southwestern University. They have over 1,000 students there. It's a really nice college. You can start something, and if it has the right direction, it does wonderful things.

Even though we have television and movies, there's no substitute for real live art. I don't think I'd be comfortable living in a place that didn't have that. It's an ingredient of life that is beautiful and really worthwhile. My wife and I were interested in the arts before we

113

came to Napa. Actually, 15 years before we came here, we founded the Conservatory in Palo Alto.

We found a live art specialty—the Zarzuela—which is enough to build a festival on. It's an impressive art form that has been almost totally unknown in this country. It is like Broadway theater, with one exception: you have opera singers instead of Broadway singers. Serious composers composed the music. It's more operatic, more serious, but at the same time more fun. To help the revival of Zarzuela, we translate the spoken parts into English. Then, we put much more emphasis on the music than on the spoken parts. With that, it becomes a very, very beautiful and modern experience.

I always think in terms of education, so we think of the Conservatory as a school. We do operas and other works of art, but primarily the orientation is toward teaching. We're doing two things: we're educating the performers and we're educating the audience. One mission is to teach young artists more about what they're interested in—their music, their language—to be in a program, to dance and to sing, to be a performer. But it is not art for art's sake. We perform for our live audience here in Napa and for the other audience who sees our works on our videos. Our other mission, then, is to help our audience learn more about opera and about this particular genre of opera. A lot of people now would see a Zarzuela who hadn't even heard the word and wouldn't have set foot in an opera house four years ago. That is our second mission.

The idea of sponsorship grows out of our dual mission. Why not bring these people together—the people who make the music and the people who appreciate the music—and develop more of a relationship, more of a bond? It seems like a no-lose situation.

We take mostly college graduates and work on their community involvement. We're the next step towards professionalism beyond the schools, because it's a big leap from the college stage to the professional stage. We just barely pay their expenses while they're here, but we give them an opportunity to learn. If we had more resources, we would sponsor them better, but right now we do what we can—we give them the education that they want, and we give them a venue at our theater. That's far more important to these artists than money.

Right now, our sponsorship is just a relationship, just personal. If these artists develop more friends here in Napa, more sponsors, it seems to me that it would be a great experience for the families here in Napa, and it would give the singers that come here a home. They come here for a month. They are intensely vibrant artists. And they look upon the Conservatory as their alma mater, a place they can come back to. If we can enlarge that to the city of Napa, and get the families of Napa to develop a relationship with these artists, it can add tremendous potential in directions that we can't even imagine.

These young artists want someone that they can write letters to, and say, "Look, I made it to the Met." "Look, I made it to the San Jose Opera." "I'm here in Germany and the audience loves me." These people want someone to be interested in them. In the short time that we've had this going, we've had several hundred artists come through here, and my wife and I get letters from most of them. They want someone to be interested in their career. And I consider that a rare, beautiful experience on my own part.

In mounting a production, you build community. On one level, people sitting alone in their houses watching TV may be getting culture and entertainment, but they're not getting a sense of community. In community theater, the people in the production have much more of a sense of community. That is really the essence of the rationale for having art to begin with—local, real, live art. It carries a lot more inspiration for young people if they can see somebody actually producing art, seeing that it is possible that they themselves produce art, as opposed to being merely passive watchers of TV.

There is a tremendous difference between producing something and presenting something. A lot of places bring in productions. People come in, take the proceeds of the gate with them, and leave. That's it. It provides entertainment, but it doesn't build anything. When you produce something, you start building things. You get electricians, stagehands who know their jobs, and carpenters who know how to build sets. You get directors, choreographers, and coaches that teach the Spanish dances. You can get singers that are on their way to becoming professional, and let them take longer, study more, with more coaching, more choreography, more rehearsing, and you can do an almost professional level of performance. In some ways, you can make it better, because you have a longer time to put it all together. When you build up this body of know-how, you have so much more, then, to work with in the future, as opposed to just bringing in something that goes away. The important thing that producers provide for a community is actually the building of a community. And that's where we're putting our emphasis—on being a producer.

It's hard work producing things. It involves a lot of detail, particularly if you try to do it really well. But through these productions, the Conservatory impacts two communities and brings them together. One is the community of artists that we're bringing into Napa and then sending back out to the world. But we stay in touch with them, so they become part of our lives. The other is the Napa community. They're pulled into this community of artists. A community relationship between these two groups of people can be nurtured. And some of the people in Napa become part of the arts community too. You lift up rocks in Napa, and great sopranos or baritones jump out. It's a wonderful discovery.

You can start something, and if it has the right direction, it does wonderful things.

The White Barn: Community as a Work of Art

by Nancy Garden

The dream of the White Barn started in 1973, when my husband David and I and our five children moved from the East Coast to the Napa Valley. On our property was an old carriage house, built in the 1870s; it had accompanied an old Victorian home that burned in the 1930s. The carriage house was structurally sound but needed a lot of work to make it usable. We did extensive renovations, keeping the building's form and mood. To our great surprise, the barn had great acoustics. Eureka! The White Barn was born! Obviously it isn't an ultra-modern BIG CITY structure, but a rural setting with an intimate atmosphere.

My goal was to offer the Barn to the community as a cultural outlet. I wanted it to serve art in the broadest sense. For a number of years we presented two or three events a year, gratis, to the community. By 1985 I was recruiting artists from throughout the Bay Area, including a fair sampling of local talent, always insisting they be paid for their work. We don't ask a plumber to work for free!

I have always felt art offers not only an outlet for creativity but is also good "therapy" for those performing and receiving. I look at art to instill beauty in a world at times gone mad. My favorite quote is by Martin Luther: "Music is a discipline, a mistress of order and good manners. She makes the people milder, gentler, more moral, and more reasonable."

It hasn't been easy creating my dream. For many years I struggled with the county government over permits. Wineries were presenting art shows and musicians in concert, so they linked my usage with theirs. Finally, Temporary Event Licenses were created, and I now can present 12 events per year.

One of my cherished memories of the valley is "Valley Pie Jubilee." I thought we should celebrate our Bicentennial musically and took my idea of a musical based on the history of our valley to City Fathers and organizations who might be interested. Vintage Hall, the precursor of Napa Valley Museum, agreed to underwrite the production, with the Napa Valley Heritage Fund underwriting any losses. Kenn Long, a local playwright and composer, was commissioned along with Bill Stafford, music arranger, Waldemar Johannsen, set designer, Orlin Koehn, set construction, Ken Rossi, graphic designer. All these professionals agreed to work for a mere stipend. Kenn and I held auditions, hoping to have at least 15 to 20 people in the cast. Seventy people auditioned and Kenn was so grateful he took them all! He rewrote the script to include ages 4 to 74. The oldest was Connie Debly, who became our own Billy Burke. People still remember her standing center stage with her magic wand transforming our ordinary valley into the Land of Oz. Incidentally, we netted $11,000 on the show.

I think the greatest thing the Barn has done is to bring people together. Performers—both amateur and professional—it's given them a venue in which to perform. The audience enjoys being in a small environment. They feel they are a part of the Barn—and they are.

David and I look after the upkeep of the Barn and all proceeds go to local charities. Community is the White Barn and the White Barn is community. I think community is having a strong sense of commitment, whether it is to your church or to your neighbor. Wherever I have lived, there has been a strong sense of community. If your neighbor is sick, you take over some chicken soup. Somebody is ill, you take him or her to the doctor, this has always been a part of my life. We are our brother's keeper. You really should care for them as one of your own family. That's probably key.

I just produced a little musical and I had some people in the cast I don't agree with politically, and they don't agree with me. But that was all right, we came together in music. I have always thought when you are involved in music, you have to be cooperative. You have to bend. You have to be flexible because you have a lot of different personalities, and a lot of different temperaments, so you learn to go with the flow. For me, music is a binding factor in the community.

Artists have to rise above the political. The show is the most important thing. They completely get out of themselves. When I play the piano, I'm not playing the piano. I'm listening to what's going on onstage. I'm at one with the singer. We have to work together. If we don't, we are not going to get a very nice sound. We're not going to get our message across.

To make music together, you have to communicate with that person. It's a very intimate relationship. Accompanying is a whole different thing from performing. When you are performing alone, you're in control. What you say comes forth. But when you're accompanying someone, their wishes, their interpretation is what you follow. What we want with community is to talk soulfully to the next person. With our soul. Not to just make conversation, as one would at a cocktail party. We really want to express ourselves. You have to keep some things small and intimate, that's what we have done with the White Barn. Maybe that's how our communities need to be, small and intimate.

Celebration of Community

by James Pratt

A fall Saturday, late morning in Indian summer.

The setting is an open space—really an underdone parking lot—in front of the low facade of a modest restaurant called Thailana, set far back from the street, bordered on one side by the brick wall of a one-story store and on the other by a small open-air shed. The area is filling with people.

In the center of the open space 150 chairs have been set up in front of a raised platform with its back toward the street. The platform holds four rows of nine chairs each. There is a microphone.

For this event, Bryan Street, named for the founder of this city, has been cordoned off from traffic. In the streetcar age this street was an important link between parts of the city, but now it has been cut, and this portion is in the process of becoming a different kind of street, a short, quiet one linking three neighborhood parks and the open space we stand in. It also ties two tiny neighborhood convenience centers into the pedestrian environment. They are rehabilitated by the infusion of immigrants and their entrepreneurship. In one of these tiny centers an excellent Thai restaurant contributes to American cuisine its noodles, curries, hot pots, and a wonderful desert of special "sticky rice" under fresh mangoes. In the other a Chinese restaurant offers soft-shell crabs that can compete with ones in Shanghai or Hong Kong. Thailana here before us serves a flavorful if picante coconut soup.

But today many of the foods are otherwise prepared. Under the shed at one side of the space, and around the edge of the open area are tables laden with foods not only from the Orient, but Latin

America and Texas. Women are heating tortillas, while Thai cooks
are carrying foil-covered pans of hot imperial rolls. Some make a con-
cession to their buyer's tastes by offering hot dogs as well as tacos and
frijoles refritos. At one side, there are market gardeners, Cambodian
farmer immigrants, selling just-picked boktoy, Chinese cabbages, and
lemon grass. These have been grown on two city lots—communal lots—
four blocks away. The lots, luxuriant because of farmer know-how,
support half the income of thirty families.

Signs at the tables are addressing different audiences. One of them
in Spanish offers information about a free clinic open on Saturday
mornings in a church. Another of them attracts middle-class wasps.
Persons at this table are seeking signatures for denying a zoning ordinance change. The enlisted names will be cited to the city's Planning
Commission in hopes that body will turn down the petition for change.
This petition from grocer Albertson's proposes to build a 60,000-square-
foot, big, box store on a block of land in the middle of two-story apartments built in the fifties. It is a suburban idea misplaced. The Idaho
chain would displace 350 residents from the block in question, and
more surrounding it. The director of the city's Planning (read: *real
estate development*) Department has approved the change without
consulting the neighborhood affected. The men and women at this
booth show plans and an image of affordable housing instead of the
formidable big box in its sea of parking. At first these wasps seem a
little out of place, but then, they are a part of the mix of city dwellers
that surround this site, only they are from across the tracks as it were,
three blocks south.

From one perspective, the wasps are responding to a "Not in my
backyard" reaction to change that would destabilize the area and force
new traffic patterns. But all surrounding neighborhoods oppose this
threat of sixteen acres of retail set down in their midst. (Albertson's
would claim only six; the land speculation and absentee ownership
surrounding would put ten more in jeopardy.) The immediate neighborhood would have to suffer eighteen-wheelers and a hundred other
trucks on this quiet Bryan Street, because the requested site backs up
to Bryan. It would kill the nearby small shops dependent on a pedestrian environment, overload by sixty percent the traffic on a narrow
street leading to the primary school, and jeopardize the work of a
dozen years to build a new kind of neighborhood here.

A health van parked in Bryan Street behind the space filling with people has been brought to offer mammograms.

Around the food stands school musicians are milling about, dressed in copies of epauletted nineteenth-century military garb, all yellow and gold or red and black, their cylindrical and billed hats balanced on the backs of their heads, chin straps akimbo. Their postures are charmingly out of sync with these operatic costumes. Their instruments are not in sight.

Children endlessly weave through clusters of people who, in the past, have not been expected in this city, in the middle of the United States on the edge of the southern plains. As they game, the children inspect foods being sold and dart for funds from their adult protectors. Some of the children from Laos or Cambodia or Vietnam are more reserved than those from Latin America and African countries.

Two policemen observe while perched on their bicycles, two others sit astride horses. The bicyclists have come from the Police Store Front two blocks up Bryan. The neighborhood association bought one of the bicycles to help get the policemen out of cars. For the past seven years in their new site, the police have brought a new and positive kind of community center to the area, where before their post was only a necessary one for security. It is a friendly place to address problems. Mothers do not have to ask as often to have drug needles cleaned up around park benches. No longer are the bodies of youths found off Bryan Street with ice-picks stirred inside their brains.

One huddle of people near the steps to the raised platform is of politicians networking assiduously.

Another huddle near the steps is of mothers and schoolteachers grooming chosen children of all ages for presentation.

People trickle to seats in the warm sunshine, both in the audience and on the platform. Three city councilpersons sit on the third row back at one end. Neighborhood leaders sit on the other end.

Principals and teachers receiving awards sit on the back row. Places are reserved in front for the United States District Attorney, the Federal District Court Judge, the U.S. Congressional Representative, and the city's Chief of Police.

A square-jawed, sandy-haired man with fine, laughing crowfoot lines beside his eyes hovers. He is a former police officer, a Vietnam veteran, and is founder and leader of the Blue Dragons, an Explorer Scout troop of primarily Southeast Asian youth. Acting as Major Domo, he directs, shepherds the various participants toward a ceremony. It is he who has fashioned this event, the third such beginning.

A bugle calls. The Blue Dragons in their uniforms assemble, march across between the platform and audience to present the flag, but then fade away.

The Major Domo comes to the microphone, tapping it to begin the proceedings. He explains that this event will combine the spring-time Inner City Life Festival (rained out last April) and the Ceremony of the Harvest Moon. It will celebrate new citizens and honor children and youth. He explains, in many Asian countries the adults give respect to their youth and children in a specific festival. Today, a committee of volunteers has raised the money from many neighborhood groups, individuals, and local businesses to mount this combined festival.

A choir of twenty police officers in white gloves rises to the plat-form. Standing at attention and full of rich baritone harmonies, they render the national anthem. They make it stirring.

A beautiful young woman dressed in gold with a bare midriff, under a tall, spiked crown with golden earflaps comes stately forward from the rear of the audience toward the platform. Her dress glints almost painfully in the bright noon sunlight as she dances and slowly advances. She carries a chalice filled with gold glitter. As she ascends the platform, her hands in lithe movements scatter glitter while the breeze obligingly wafts it toward the audience. We seemingly have been blessed as this goddess retreats back through the audience and disappears into Thailana. Is this golden apparition incongruous in this community setting that lacks most forms of decorum? Or is she a harbinger of some new order? She brings a kind of serene dignity, unique to this American setting.

Food continues to be sold at the surrounding tables. The foods come from the Parent-Teachers' Associations of fifteen surrounding inner-city schools. The city has waved rental costs under the shed so that all the proceeds from each table will go to its school.

Some waiting participants seek shade under the shed. It is not large enough for this event. It has been built because ten years ago an urban designer saw a need for physical centers to organize civic life in a great amorphous region of the abandoned inner city. An immigrant care-provider told this planner that immigrants brought to this neigh-borhood needed a place for business incubation, to exploit their skills by trading goods they could make while they acquired English. Eight years ago the City Council agreed, but only to build a small piece of the planned community center.

The Major Domo introduces the local School Board Representative to the crowd. This elected Representative, a smiling, single mother of five, fluent in Spanish, convenes the event in two languages. (There have been other events where translators had to be present for five languages. Some have been left out today.) She is heavily supported by the area PTAs, because she fought to end busing for their children. Almost singlehandedly through her PTA leadership, she caused two new grade schools for 2,400 primary students to be built in this neighborhood in the past six years. With the help of one church she has established on-going English classes for immigrant wives, successful because she remembered to supply child care and hold classes during the day when wives are not required to attend husbands at home.

She proclaims this Ceremony of the Harvest Moon will not only honor children and youth, but also principals and teachers from the fifteen inner-city schools.

She explains that there has been a contest among 250 volunteer students, for prizes in writing an essay. The contest required the participants to express their thoughts on "How you see unity through diversity." She will introduce the winners of the contest from kindergarten through eighth grade. (Kindergartners expressed their concepts in painting or drawing.) The contest explained, and the prizes proclaimed for each grade level as two $50 awards and certificates, the students one-by-one come forward to climb the stairs to the platform and be introduced, honored as it were, then receive their rewards.

Their eyes and brightness hearteningly shine through complexions of all shades. Their obvious excellence as individuals, as ardent learners, as contributors, causes a lump in the throat.

She then recognizes the contributions of principals and teachers.

The School Board Representative introduces the U.S. Congressional Representative, a handsome African-American woman. She in turn introduces the U.S. District Attorney and the Chief of Police, the latter a friendly, smiling, but taut man in a tightly tailored, dress-black uniform ornamented in silver. These two laud the "Weed and Seed" program in effect in the area. Finally the Federal District Judge, also in black, but flowing robe, is introduced.

Suddenly a bailiff in clarion voice almost shouts for all to rise, jerking us to our feet, proclaiming, "Hear Ye, Hear Ye!! The United

States District Court is in session, the Honorable Judge presiding! The Judge declares Court open for the purposes of swearing in 101 new citizens of the United States.

He tells candidate citizens, not individually but by country of origin, to rise as their birthland is called. The countries are not organized by alphabet, but by region. First is one person from Korea, then the Philippines, the various Southeast Asian countries. Then India, Iran, Israel, Russia, and Eastern European countries. Ethiopia sends a very blonde candidate—there are no stereotypes. Nigeria, South Africa, Portugal, and finally the Americas. Of course, Mexico is the most represented, but there are at least singles from most every country of the new world, including Canada. There must be persons from 45 countries here, but none from European, developed, first-world countries.

The Judge speaks.

The Judge administers the oath of citizenship. The 101 give up any allegiance to foreign potentates, and swear to uphold the Constitution. He pronounces the 101 candidates, having completed all requirements, now to be citizens. He declares Court adjourned. There is a great clapping, and everyone smiles as they line up to receive verification.

The U.S. Congresswoman admonished the new citizens to participate in government, to make certain to vote. She states that she herself did not understand that importance until she was out of college.

As the chairs on the podium are cleared for the next event, a large dragon carried over six black legs appears. Four persons in black also flank the dragon—or is it an oriental lion? It is made of painted wood and canvas, and has been created by a college-student organization. One senses it contains many symbols of a Southeast Asian culture. The head bobs up and down, and from side to side, as the animal advances from the rear of the shed into the open area. It must be very heavy, as from time to time one of the accompanying students in black slips under the body and takes over maneuvering the head. As the creature moves, the middle and rear legs continually collide with each other and the head.

Meanwhile, the ceremony moves off the platform to a microphone below, where the Federal Judge, Congressional Representative, and the two City Councilpersons representing the surrounding neighborhoods hand out individual certificates of citizenship, congratulating each recipient.

Up on the podium behind, the Major Domo announces first a dance with bamboo poles. Next, four women in long, hand-dyed, cotton skirts maintain perfect perpendicular carriage as they dance. They must, or they will spill the glasses of water set atop their heads. Their motions balance perfectly; no water migrates from the glasses. Then a group of student flamenco dancers in traditional slit and flounced red skirts, with youths in black pork-pie hats arrive. Behind the shed, bands are assembling.

Marching bands come forward, and entertainment continues through the balmy fall afternoon.

The tables still dispense food to a great range of tastes. The odors, sounds, languages, and colors intermingle, moving beyond political discord as an expression of true community.

Building community is not a fast process. The churches have done their quiet work in the area around this space to bring English classes—in one run-down apartment one can find, for example, a Vietnamese Colonel and his family sitting with two women from Somalia and four persons from Nicaragua in a class of nine. In the closest grade school, a group of "co-madres" meets with the help of another minister translating Spanish.

A group of churches and the YWCA has hosted the fledgling neighborhood group for seven years; before that the urban designer hosted meetings for five years. The resident private foundation has contributed a children's park and a youth soccer field. The neighborhood organization has held focus groups among Hispanics, Asians, and local businesses to clarify community needs. Even the Blue Dragon Scout Troop has helped security by installing peep-holes in many apartment doors of the area.

Care-providers here twelve years ago also requested more housing, housing that immigrants could afford. That process only just begins. The neighborhood organization has blown on sparks to create its own fire for ten years, and now it catches. It has become recognized by the city as a Community Housing Development Organization, with power to buy, sell, and own real estate. It has gotten the city to award it drug-seized and tax-delinquent properties as two candidates for new housing. A private foundation has given it two properties on which to build. It has acquired a revolving fund loan with which to negotiate for other properties. Operating funds have come. A neighboring community organization has loaned it funds. The State

Legislative Representative who lives in one adjacent neighborhood is helping with state loans. The Albertson's challenge has brought several communities together. Their work is far from finished. Rather than continue to be an immigrant way station, this community would keep a portion of its new dwellings for sale to new citizens of low and modest income—most especially those who now live there—but do so in a manner to attract market-rate homes as well for middle-income persons. Better housing would bring back persons who started their American life here. With its new housing mix, the community would recall the fine-grained income diversity, the smaller scale, mixed variety in housing stock built before World War II. And when the City Council repulses the Albertson's attack on the neighborhood, the community dreams of building 120 homes on that tract to reinforce the pedestrian character of Bryan Street, and other streets feeding its primary schools. It has an ideal inner-city location, already speculated in for future real estate appreciation. Can this community guide investment enough to prevent a laissez-faire market from harming a sense of community that is inclusive of more than one income group, more than one immigrant or ethnic group?

This immediate inner-city neighborhood, lost in drug wars for twenty years and housing the poorest in per-capita income of any area in the city, suddenly shows unique promise. On a parking lot and under a city shed, however nascent, it has created a community center. The interface between people of several cultures has become more possible. No longer hidden, community has taken on a positive public stance. Hence, America, the United States, and this city have become richer by the presence of these children, most of them of immigrant parents, being publicly rewarded, and by the pledge of 101 individuals from so many countries before their peers.

Community and Carnival

by Kirk J. Schneider

The fluid center* of the Napa Valley community is a vibrant, throbbing, alive center. It is constituted by three basic elements: choice, intersecting possibility, and cohesion or structure. These three elements, it seems to me, promote peak aliveness in human beings, peak awareness. Furthermore, they optimally acknowledge our greatness, vastness before creation, as well as that of our smallness, insignificance.

Napa's communal fluid center is therefore both bold and humble. It is a pivot point, a pause, a flexible base upon which to dwell. The fluid center implies discovery, adventure, innovation, but it also recognizes needs for safety, support, and unity.

The metaphor of carnival: This notion of festival, of multifaceted circus and ritual, beautifully captures the Napa Valley ethos. Carnival reflects the literary perspective more than it does the philosophical. As such it reflects art more than science, play more than analysis. The distinguishing feature of carnival as found here in Napa is its *generosity*. It promotes empathy, identification with otherness, discovery. Yet carnival is *not* anarchy. It is not "anything goes" nor is it fanatically egalitarian. By contrast, carnival is an "ordered playfulness," as one writer recently put it. There is room for everyone at the carnival except those who would seek to destroy it, that is, those who would injure, loot, or plunder its celebrants. There is no room for homogenizing carnival, either by eradicating its safety, support, and cohesion or by

---

* A fuller version of this concept can be found in *The Humanistic Psychologist* (in press), the official journal of the Humanistic Psychology Division of the American Psychological Association.

annihilating its adventurousness, boldness, and innovation. There is no room for either pervasive greatness or total smallness at carnival.

Carnival is a live and let live forum. There is room for the flamboyant and room for the understated. There is room for the disabled and room for the robust at carnival. Yes, there is even room for the materialist, reductionist, and entrepreneur, so long as they don't impose themselves on others. Although I believe more open and integrative participants in carnival—those that embody carnival itself—are the more rewarding groups, I do not believe we should imply that *only* open and integrative types are welcome. Such a view would not only be naïve, it would be limiting of the nature most of us share. We must hold a place, it seems to me, for the many parts of ourselves, including those that are ambitious, rivalrous, or fragmentary.

Once immersed in carnival, one would have less and less reason to polarize from or destroy that which is "other." While otherness could still be frightening, anxiety provoking, or puzzling to one, it would be an ever-present reality at carnival and therefore intimately woven into one's experience.

So the great question, of course, is how has Napa translated this notion of carnival and the fluid center into everyday reality? Let me propose a few responses of my own to provide a stimulus. The first principle that the Napa philosophy embodies, is acknowledgment of both greatness and smallness, concerns about mattering, but not too much (!), in the practical application of people's desires. Napa has a citizenry and culture that go hand in hand, that are fluid, but that respect the integrity of the whole. If it were otherwise, if Napa were polarized, it would turn out individuals who either grandstand or shrink away from challenges.

The deeper question for those of us who would like to take Napa to our own communities is a personal one—how much do we live and breathe the legacy of carnival in our own lives? How willing are we to take a *stand* for this view, despite the forces eroding it?

The Opera House and the Oxbow School

by Margrit Biever Mondavi

The Opera House

The Opera House project actually began with my friend, Veronica diRosa. Veronica and I were very close. I found her very elfin, almost European. Then we found that we both loved art.

We were always interested in the town of Napa. I lived there for about 20 years. In fact our residence has a Napa address today. I saw what happened to Napa. There was defoliation: There was the taking down of the old houses, there were suddenly one-way streets—that were not necessary because nobody came anyway, and they tore up the houses to put in parking garages—for what? When nobody came. They had no soul or understanding of history. I thought, where is this insanity going to lead us? And after they had built the tower and the mall down the middle of the town and half of the shops were empty—then the outlet mall was put by the freeway. So, of course, everybody went shopping there—that brings a million people a year. And then, they go back onto Highway 29, and come straight up the valley. I had written a few letters, but they didn't do any good, so we thought, "Let's start with something to revive the city." And that's how it started.

The Opera House in downtown Napa had a lovely façade, and we both felt that it would be a home for performing arts, in which we were interested. The sadness of it all was that it was going to be demolished by the town of Napa, and we said, "This cannot happen." We decided that restoring the theater would be a great thing to do for Napa.

The Opera House had been used from 1879 probably until the First World War. It was one of those community places they also used for graduations. It was called Opry House, like you see in places like Aspen and Nevada City. Many western towns have this kind of an Opry House, that held some recitals and community events, but was really not an *Opera* House.

In the First World War, they used it as an armory—for the storage of weapons and junk. Afterwards, they sold the chairs—there were 650 chairs—for $2 apiece. Then I think it was also a rug storage place, all kinds of things. And finally, the rats and the vermin ate it up. It was a complete rathole. It was a shell. It was going to fall down. People used it as a toilet. You can't imagine how horrible it was.

It took a lot of imagination. The first thing we did when we started to raise a little money, was redo the façade (a very lovely façade), and then came the big scaffolding. In the meantime, we got architects to design the inside of it. The performing stage will be on the second floor, and on the first floor we'll have cafes and shops, so it will be used daily, and there will be a more river development on that side.

When we got the front up, rebuilt and resplendent, we had a street dance. We were able to close Main Street for an hour and a half. We had performers on the street, and everybody danced.

Veronica was a wonderful artist, and a wonderful soul. She was kind and gentle and humble, and she had this great *joie de vivre*. Before she went to France, from where she never came back—two days before—we had breakfast at ABC and planned it out, what was going to happen with the Opera House. And then, when she fell off the cliff and died, her husband Rene called me in England. I made all the arrangements to meet him, but at the last moment Rene called to say that he had taken care of all the formalities and was on his way home. I can never believe that she's gone. The people who were involved in the Opera House took it on as Veronica's legacy. Every time we have an event, I always say it's for Veronica. Veronica's going to see that her dream has come true, because I believe that she knows what's going on from her special cloud in heaven.

Bob decided to put in $2 million, with a bonus if it could be matched by the end of this year. He did that for me. He said, "I want Margrit's name on something."

And what's going to make it go I think is that it's now in the triumvirate of the American Center and the Oxbow School. It's magic that this has happened.

The Oxbow School

Bob is giving his money away. I said, "An art school would be, for me, a dream." Ann Hatch, who did the Cap Street Project in San Francisco, where they do these installations for artists that need the space, came to us and said, "We have this idea." We immediately said, "You've got to come to Napa." First, we went to Andover, near Boston, to look at a prep school that was very art oriented. The Arts Chair at Andover, Chuck Reynolds, promised to come on our board, which he did. So there was already a great exchange.

So, we donated $6 million. Ann donated $4 million. It's so good! Stanley Seidowitz, who is the Architectural Chair at Berkeley, and designed Ann's house in San Francisco and her cottage in Sebastopol, which is very modern, and which I love, is designing the three studios. One is a double studio and two are single studios. The City Council said, "Cancel it." We shmoozed all five council members. I invited them to the winery for lunch. They were in unison that the site was a Victorian surrounding, that we should honor it. But it's a junky street down there. There was the fairgrounds, and all these low-income houses, and the trailer park by Vallergas. It's not very attractive. Seidowitz had designed the three studios using a lot of glass bricks with an open view to the river, and the council was against the glass bricks. We had to make some compromises. We bought some surrounding buildings. Some of them were apartment houses and we were able to make dorms out of them and some are faculty housing. Some had interesting local history which we respected and researched. Plaques are in front of these houses describing their building date and past inhabitants. The gardens are going to be for the children to plant, to be conscious of the environment.

Finally, what saved the design—the night before the vote, KQED, our public television station, broadcast a program on the life of Frank Lloyd Wright, and one of the members saw the program. She called me that morning and said, "You know what, Margrit? I'm going to vote for it." It passed, 3 to 2.

My involvement with the school now is the joy of seeing it come about. I go visit it, and I'm jealous. To be a child, to be a student again, with three or four artists in residence who surround you and really guide you, and we have all the other subjects—there is English and math and science. I want to be a resident!

VI
The
Business
of
Community

Community and Excellence

by Robert Mondavi

I was brought up always wanting to excel. It's very simple. I stopped at nothing to excel in winemaking. Winemaking is a living thing. Each and every year is different. Perhaps we had a very cold spring. We might have an extremely hot summer. Well, the grapes that grow here will be different. So, we have to understand that it's not like steel plate, or something that you can manufacture. This is a living thing. It changes each and every year, so there's a challenge to understand the grapes. But you can have that love and desire, whether you grow grapes or wheat or vegetables. You can get the same passion.

Because we wanted to excel in wine and food, we met Julia Child and Dick Graff who were also interested in wine and food, and we formed the American Institute of Wine and Food about 18 years ago. What was it for? To enhance the quality of life. I realized that I was fortunate. My mother was an excellent cook. I didn't know how good she was until we brought three-star chefs from France over here. Then I said, "Wait a minute!" My mother's food was all natural, and very good. No excess butter and creams or things like that.

Another thing I want to do—I have always wanted to give something back to the community. It's just that simple. Margrit taught me the importance of art, and we've had art programs ever since. In fact, in the early 60s when we were at the Charles Krug winery, she came to me one time to have a program for the community. So we started with a little program—August Moon Concerts. It was a benefit for young audiences, to bring music to grade-school children that had no idea what a conductor or an oboe was.

We can destroy this community, or we can make it more beautiful. It's very important that we have a master plan for the county and
the city. Otherwise, we'll have people coming in and destroying this
whole thing. That's the one thing I'm very worried about. I've been
working hard—we are still trying to get certain key business people
together to set up a master plan for the county and yet allow each
of the cities to work independently. We want to get Calistoga, St.
Helena, Yountville, Rutherford, Oakville, and Napa working in harmony for the benefit of the whole community. If we don't do that,
developers will come in and before you know it we'll be a mishmash.
If a developer comes in without the right program, then you could
have a mishmash that is not going to reflect what we want here. It
takes leadership. There are many things that are developing, that if
we don't watch that, we can destroy what we have here.

If you were to come to me and ask, "What should I do in my
community . . ." I would say, "Excel." And I would give you the 15
points from my book, *Harvests of Joy*. These ideas apply to leadership, personal growth, and building a community. I'll repeat them
here for you.

*First and foremost you must have confidence and faith in
yourself.*

*Second, whatever you choose to do, make a commitment to
excel, and then pour yourself into it with your heart and soul and
complete dedication.*

*Third, interest is not enough—you must be passionate about
what you do if you want to succeed and have a happy life. Find a job
you love and you'll never have to work a day in your life.*

*Fourth, establish a goal just beyond what you think you can do.
When you achieve that, establish another and another. This will
teach you to embrace risk.*

*Fifth, be completely honest and open. I never had secrets. I
would share my knowledge and experience with others if they would
share with me. I always had confidence that there was enough room
for all of us.*

*Sixth, generosity pays. So learn to initiate giving. What you
give will enrich your life and come back to you many times over.*

*Seventh, only make promises and commitments you know you can
keep. A broken promise can damage your credibility and reputation
beyond repair.*

Eighth, you must understand that you cannot change people. It took me a long time to learn that. You might be able to influence them a little, but you can't change anyone but yourself. So accept people the way they are. Accept their differences and try to work with them as they are. I learned this late in life, and it is amazing what peace of mind I found when I finally understood it.

Ninth, to live and work in harmony with others, don't be judgmental. Instead, cultivate tolerance, empathy, and compassion. And never berate people, especially your children, in front of their cohorts. I used to think I could talk to my children, lay the cards on the table—"Don't forget to do that. I know. This is better." You should speak to them individually. *Otherwise this can be dispiriting and damaging to them, and it's counterproductive. As I've learned, if you want to teach someone to fly, you don't start by clipping his wings.*

Tenth, human beings experience the same thing in very different ways. Two people can live through the exact same experience and come away with totally different understandings of what happened. So between people there is always a large space for misunderstanding. Always be alert for misunderstandings and tread lightly, especially when it comes to politics, religion, or moral standards. You learn that when you travel the world over.

Eleventh, it is very important that we understand one another. We need to learn how to bridge those spaces of misunderstanding. To do this, listen carefully, and when you talk, be sure people understand you. On important issues, have people repeat back to you what you've said, to make sure there are no areas of confusion or conflict. My brother and I—we thought we understood, but we didn't understand each other. That's why I was very careful with my own children to repeat things. And that's why we're still together. You need every bit of that understanding to make a relationship work.

Twelfth, rarely will you find complete harmony between two human beings. But if you find it, maintaining this harmony requires individuals or soul mates to have complete confidence in one another. Make time to be alone, to share experiences and appreciate together precious moments and the beauty of life. Open all of yourself to that person—emotionally, physically, spiritually, and intellectually. And always, always leave time for playfulness and laughter. There is no better tonic for keeping love alive and vibrant than laughter and good cheer.

Thirteenth, in both life and work, stay flexible. Whether in a country, a company, or a family, the same holds true: Dictatorship and rigidity rarely work. Freedom and elasticity do.

Fourteenth, always stay positive. Use your common sense. There are a lot of intelligent people, but few with common sense. *And remember this: America was built on the can-do spirit and will continue to thrive on the can-do spirit.*

Fifteenth, out of all the rigidities and mistakes of my past, I've learned one final lesson, and I'd like to see it engraved on the desk of every business leader, teacher, and parent in America: The greatest leaders don't rule. They inspire.

I strongly believe our country should be known not only for its strength and technology, but also for its culture, quality of life, and its civilization. What has made our company different from others is that we always believed in associating wine with food and the arts to enhance the quality of our life. I never wanted to sell boxes, I wanted to sell quality and the enhancement in the quality of our life.

For this reason I am beginning the American Center for Wine, Food, and the Arts in Napa, which will be unique in the world and which will be a place of international renown. It will focus on the variety of cultural achievements in this country, including those made by our chefs and winemakers. It will be available as an educational resource for all those interested in the finer things in life—the good life. It is a $70-million operation—we broke ground last June and the center plans to open on Thanksgiving 2001.

I have been fortunate to receive, now I want to give something back to our community, our country, our way of life.

Making Community Your Business

by Brian Kelly

In 1978, I was working for the Bank of America in Oakland. There was an opening for somebody to manage the wine industry for BofA in the North Bay. I jumped at the job and got it. At that time, a fellow by the name of Andy Johnson was the manager of the Bank of America in St. Helena. He came in as assistant manager around 1960 and was there for about 22 years. In fact, the bank was affectionately known as the Bank of Andy Johnson. That bank had the fastest growing, most profitable, cleanest portfolio of any branch of BofA in northern California. The only branch in northern California that made more money than we did was the San Francisco main branch. Why was that? Because Andy was involved in the community. One reason we were successful from a business point of view was that we were accepted into the wine industry. At that time, Price Waterhouse, and other accounting firms put on forums each year. And the Wine Institute held regular meetings. We went to all those forums and immersed ourselves in getting to know the wine industry. We were the only bank there. The reward was that we banked 90% of their business.

No other bank recognized the secret. They didn't go to the conferences. If you go to a wine industry conference now, there are more bankers and financial people there than there are winery people, but in the late 70s and through the middle of the 80s, that was not the case. That taught me something: If you really want to get into a community, you've got to immerse yourself in it and get to know it. If you know the community, then you can do a better job. That's part of what we've done at Napa National Bank—we've gotten into the community.

When I came to Napa National Bank, the bank was not very well known. Name recognition was poor. We were not immersed in the community at all. It struck me that we were paying a public relations firm $40,000 a year for PR and marketing, and we had not grown an inch in five years. Taking a lesson from the Bank of Andy Johnson, I realized that we needed to get into the community, understand the community, find out what it's about, and get ourselves known in the community. That strategy, I thought, would have some rewards. At the time, we had 30 employees. One employee was on the symphony board, and one was in Rotary, and that was it. That was the extent of the bank's involvement in the community.

There was another bank here in town called Napa Valley Bank. Napa Valley Bank was at all the fairs. Napa Valley Bank was donating $250,000 in cash to the community each year. They were 12 to 14 times our size. We couldn't even donate $30,000 at that time. It was too expensive. I thought, "Why can't we replicate *something* that they're doing?" because they were the significant bank in this community. In the banking industry, tellers and clerical staff don't make a lot of money. So we said, "Why don't we give time instead of dollars?"

So we got involved in the community by joining organizations. It didn't happen overnight. We made some donations, but mostly the employees would volunteer to cashier at events. One way to get to know people is if you're the one who's always taking the silent auction items or handing out the tickets at a venue. A lot of people see you when you're the cashier, so we started out doing that.

One of the concerns I had in starting this program was that if I started to tell people they had to join the Rotary, and it wasn't their cup of tea, that's not going to do any good. They're not going to really jump into it. So it wasn't a requirement. There was encouragement. I allowed them the time. And it was fun for them. If I'm the boss and I give them the time, and it isn't going to cost them anything—because I pick up the tab for the service club or the events they are going to—then it is pretty easy. So I gave them the time to spend and the dollars.

At Napa National, we also recognize community service in terms of performance. We started a little program for the clerical staff. Actually, I picked this up from Vallergas, our local supermarket. One day, I happened to tell Ray Sercu, who's the president of Vallergas, "I just got great service from So-and-so. He really helped me out." Ray said, "Great. I'll give him a gold star." I said, "What's a gold star?"

He said, "It's a reward system. When they get five gold stars, they get a day off." I said, "What a great idea!" So now we're doing that. And we give stars for community activities. If our employees volunteer for an event in off-hours then we give them a gold star. It has to be an event that takes a few hours; it can't be a half-hour event. When they get five of these gold stars, they get a day off. We recognize and appreciate their being involved. And I think they appreciate being involved. Now we've got 80 employees and we're probably on 70 boards and organizations. Almost everybody is in something. If you took everybody's community hours and added them all up, it would amount to at least two if not three full-time positions.

We also have lots of community meetings at the bank. We have a great conference room, so we let other groups use it to have meetings. I love to have lunches there. It's cheaper than going to a restaurant, and people have to walk through the bank to get there. It gives to the community, but they have to walk through the bank. They have to see the bank. They say, "Oh, what a nice place . . . what nice employees." It builds community awareness.

Community involvement is directed from the top, but it has got to come from the bottom, too. You've got to have people who want to do it. For example, I interview every employee that works at the bank—even the tellers. It's not that I'm making the decision. Somebody else is making the decision to hire the people, but before they're given an offer, I interview them. It's really just to talk philosophy. I want them to say that they're buying in to what we're about and what we're trying to do.

I am making community involvement more of a requirement now for the more senior officers. We've grown dramatically, so I've brought a number of people in. Some live here; some don't. I can't always find the talent I need here, so I have to import it from Petaluma or Santa Rosa. I say, "I think every officer needs to be in some organization. I'm not going to tell you which one, but it's got to help the bank and it's got to help the community. That's what we're about." It's part of our strategic plan, one of our five tenets. We want to have (1) good control, (2) good profit, (3) good growth, (4) liquidity in the stock, and (5) community involvement.

We've gotten heavily involved in the Hispanic community. We have a significant number of Hispanic accounts and we've worked hard to get them. The Hispanics are going to be the fabric of our community and we might as well get banking them now, because they are going to grow and they're going to be a significant part of this community. So let's get all of their business. We've worked hard at doing that. I've given one employee a lot of latitude for community involvement, and she's done a great job bringing the Hispanic community to us.

Going through high school, I used to have a saying, "You can't break up a clique, you can only join it." The Hispanic community is a good example. The best thing to do is to get us all joined together. Then you have something. The Hispanic business community had a Chamber of Commerce that they were affiliated with up in Solano. It was called the Napa-Solano Hispanic Chamber of Commerce. It was totally separate from Napa's Chamber of Commerce. There was a lot of controversy about that. Now, we actually have an Hispanic division, because we want to include them in the Napa Chamber of Commerce. They want to maintain some solidarity, but they'll still come to all of the events and they'll get involved, and they'll get on various committees. That is breaking the barrier down. I think that's happening in a variety of areas in the community. There's a tremendous cross-pollination.

A large corporation can encourage community involvement too, right down to the roots. You've got to go to the local manager level. I make it simpler by allowing time off during the day and by paying for local involvement. That's a way to give without giving money directly. Maybe another way to do it is to point out the examples where there are successful branch managers out there—businesswise as well as communitywise. If that's why they've been successful in their branches, by getting to know the community, then show it off. As president of Napa National Bank, I may have an easier road than the president of a manufacturing company that doesn't really recoup the benefit. We obviously recoup benefit for being involved in the community. We're growing at about 15 percent a year.

Building Relationships

by Brad Wagenknecht

We moved to Napa when I was five years old. My dad was the youth development advisor with the University of California Cooperative Extension. The cooperative extension brings the research of the university to the local level. We grew up looking at community development as something that's important. We learned that developing people is the most important thing we can do.

I started in politics when I was in the fourth grade. Ralph Bollin, who was the pastor at a small Presbyterian church in Napa, decided he was going to run for City Council. I was in fourth grade, and I told my dad, "I want to help this guy become city councilman." Dad was friends with Ralph and he let Ralph know that I was interested. Ralph gave me a bunch of leaflets and said, "Just walk around your neighborhood." So I went and knocked on the doors in the neighborhood and gave them the leaflets.

When I was in sixth grade, we moved to Washington, D.C., because my dad was getting a Masters degree from George Washington University. He took a sabbatical, and all six of us went to Washington, D.C. We lived in an apartment, which was different for us, and I started a little newspaper there. I got hectagraph jelly—you write out your stencil, put the stencil on top of it, and the stencil lettering sticks on there. Then you put a piece of paper on, and it pulls off some ink, and put another piece of paper, and it pulls off more ink. You can print 50–100 copies. I started a neighborhood newspaper in our apartment complex that way. The people there liked having a sixth-grade kid do a newspaper. After a while, I wrote it out and they typed it up for me and printed it on mimeograph. I've done newspapers ever since.

After my wife and I got married, we found a little 800-foot house on Spencer Street, in an area called the ABC Streets. That's where my daughter was born. We were right behind the Dairy Queen—every night we'd hear, "45". . . "46". . . "47". . . as they'd call out numbers for the hamburger orders. We did a neighborhood newspaper for 10 years in that area. One of the things about doing a neighborhood newspaper is that people are a little nervous about committing if you knock on the door and ask them to come to a meeting. They say, "I don't want to come to a meeting. I don't know you." But if you leave a newspaper at their door every month, after a while, they all feel they know you, so you can get some participation. We had recipes and advice columns, and every month we'd get a number of neighbors together and do a poll—like the greatest rock and roll songs. Or I'd go buy pizzas from all the pizza places and we'd blind taste them and write down who had the best pizzas or the best chile rellenos.

The businesses around there would support the little newspaper too. It brought people together. When you have kids and they play around in the neighborhood, that brings people together. A lot of these neighborhoods—that one in particular—had a few young people scattered around, and a number of older people. It didn't have anything bringing it together. The paper brought it together. I would get calls: "We lost our skateboard. Can you put it in there and help us find it?" Or "we've got extra squash." Of course, everybody's got extra squash!

The neighborhood did all sorts of things. We had some neighborhood big dinners. We have a lot of Catholics, because it's near the Catholic Church, so the Italian Catholic buddies would make us tons of spaghetti for spaghetti dinners. One year, I raised a pumpkin vine with about 50 small pumpkins on it. You can write on a pumpkin early on and it will show up as the pumpkin grows, so I wrote all my neighbors' names on pumpkins. When we had this big dinner, I had the different pumpkins as centerpieces. I told the neighbors, "Find your own pumpkin and take it home." They loved it.

I ran for City Council when I just barely turned 30. My way of running is knocking on everybody's door and having a very simple brochure. I can honestly tell you I've never run a negative campaign. It's generally: here are my principles. Here's what I'm trying to do. And knocking on the door and spending hours and hours and hours talking to different people as you go knocking on every door. Most people just accept the leaflet and say thank you. And that's it. But a lot of people want to say stuff and want to give you an idea of what they want to see. It gives you a sense of what the Napa community is about.

When I ran in 1984, I originally lost. The night of the election, I wasn't able to watch the returns. My campaign manager and I were out taking down signs instead. There was a party back at my house, and by the time we went back there, I had lost. The top two vote-getters are elected. I ended up in fifth place. Naturally, I was disappointed. At about 11:30, after everybody had gone home, a Napa County supervisor called me and said, "You won." I said, "Come on. Don't be mean." He said, "You won. There was a computer error, and the numbers were misaligned." I was in second place when they lined it up right. I went from fifth to second. The poor guy who went from second to third—he just fell off a few votes, but it put me in front of him. He had had a victory party all night, only to hear at 11:30 that he didn't win. I spoke at his funeral a couple of years ago. I guess he had run for all sorts of things and had never won a race. I reminded everybody that he had won the election for City Council—for four or five hours.

I was on the City Council for four years. Political community involvement is like any other job. Some people are naturals at it. I have to learn. It takes me time. I had wanted to be involved in the community in this way, and here I was, where I wanted to be, but I was too nervous about everything I did—so I didn't run again for reelection. It was good for me to take some time off. Then I ran again in 1992. I've learned that I'm going to make the best decision I can. I'm a little more relaxed about it.

Leadership is risk-taking. What I try to do is have a relationship with the community. That allows me to take some risks. Whether I know you personally, or you've seen and heard what I've said over the years, you have a sense of what my mission in the community is, and what I stand for. You may disagree—and you talk about it. You tell me why you disagree and I bring up the points that I saw in it. I think most of those folks still vote for me. I've always had a good relationship with the community. Over the years, I've had hundreds of neighborhood meetings. I walk the neighborhoods when I'm running, but then I walk it during the off-time, so I can find out what's going on.

I have a survey method that has worked really nicely for me. There are times when you ask a question or take a survey because you want to know the answer. For example, when they proposed the Home Depot, I went to 20 neighborhoods and asked 50 people in each neighborhood what they thought about Home Depot. They truly wanted to have Home Depot. This was one of those times when I was willing to hear the answer. If they had said no, I would have voted against it. But over 75 percent were strongly in favor. They said, "we go out of town and do Home Depot shopping now, so why not build one here?" It was interesting talking to 1,000 people and getting their ideas on an issue that's current. I've done that for a number of items. You can't do it for all issues. In fact, you don't want to do it for all issues.

Sometimes, I don't ask a question if I don't want to hear the answer. For example, affordable housing is something that I feel is our job. As a community, we need to make sure we have places that are affordable. The magic to the Napa Valley is that we're not Marin. We have places for people who are working our fields and working at our hotels and teaching in our schools. We have places for us to live. That's one of the important things we need to keep. So, if we've found a good spot for an affordable housing project, I won't go and ask that neighborhood if they want the project. I know what their answer will be. If I hear that answer, then I have to respond to it. I know that what I have to do is make sure that the housing project is an addition to the community, not a subtraction, and then it will work out for everyone.

I think the beauty of our valley is that we have this mixture. It's that mixture that makes it vibrant. It makes it alive. I think there needs to be a valleywide vision on how to fix affordable housing, how to make housing continue to be affordable. The vision that I have is that you would be able to live and work in the same town. You'd have professional jobs and entry-level jobs, and you'd have the whole spectrum of jobs and the whole spectrum of housing. That's what I'd like to see happen. If the Bay Area did that, there'd be no traffic issue because everyone would be working in their own areas. That's what I'd like to see.

I want the community to be together. I don't have to be the bandleader, leading the community. I like to help facilitate. A good idea has a thousand parents. It's the bad idea that becomes the bastard child. You want your idea to have a thousand parents. As a government official, I sometimes get to sit up front, like we did last week when we signed for the river project, but it truly is the community that came together and did that. The question we keep asking, as part of the government, is: "Is there community involvement?" Let's keep asking the question when you come and say, "This is what we're going to do." Before we just jump and do it, let's ask, "Who have you worked with? Have you gotten this beyond just your idea? Has it become a community idea?"

I've been a teacher for 23 years in the Unified School District. For the first 10 years, I was a special ed teacher, working with emotionally disturbed adolescents for different programs in the Napa area. For the last 10 years, I've been a seventh grade social studies teacher.

Teaching is building relationships. I love teaching. When I teach an era in world history, I have costumes that I wear for the era. I walk into the room in tights, and the students don't know what to make of it. I change in the closet, and walk out, and the kids from the other classes go, "Oh, no." They think it's silly. The beauty of it is that they make me tell them why I'm dressed like that. Oh darn, I have to explain why! A teachable moment!

I teach Monday, Thursday, and Friday, and do the supervisor work the other days and the evenings. I think both jobs are complicated. You have to have a vision for the future for both teaching and community leadership. If you don't have a vision for what you want the community to be like, you shouldn't be in either one of those jobs.

Lessons for the Community
from the Business Perspective

by Dana Leavitt

Napa County needs to be looked at as one community, rather than five separate cities and a county administration. Everything that happens in one of the cities ultimately has an impact on all of the others. The whole county needs to recognize that. Then we can put together a master plan for the county that says, "Here are some ways the housing shortages might be handled. Here are some things we can do about transportation. Here's how we can protect the agriculture."

To get things done in the community, it takes the community to do it. You can't delegate that responsibility to just the elected officials. Politicians are never going to provide the vision, the long-term objectives. They're not going to take the risks. They have too many varied constituencies to try to represent. They've got too many reasons for them not to do it. Every day, you read in the paper about some community that has taken dramatic steps to change the community. It isn't the elected politicians that have done it. It's people who do it, and in many instances, they are successful despite the politicians.

The cooperative thinking and attitudes that succeeded in developing a plan to manage the flooding of the Napa River can also be used to develop a master plan that will benefit Napa County. One essential element of the flood control process was compromise. The development of that plan was one of the first times in anybody's memory that all the cities in Napa County—Calistoga, St. Helena, Yountville, Napa, and American Canyon—came together and worked on a common problem, and solved it with compromise, so that no one ended up with everything, but all of them ended up with enough of what they

148

wanted. Every mayor approved the plan. Every City Council approved it. It was an incredible accomplishment. People in the community who had definite ideas realized that the only way anything was going to get accomplished was through elements of compromise. The Army Corps of Engineers gave up a lot of their usual requirements. The Friends of the River agreed to put aside some of the things they wanted. The Sierra Club made compromises. Fish and Game did. The cities did. Everybody did, recognizing that if we insist on everything we think has to be done, nothing is going to happen.

There were a series of meeting with sometimes a couple hundred people involved, representatives from all these different entities. They could see when a group of maybe ten people were holding out for one specific demand. Suddenly there would be 150 people saying, "You can't get that. We're all giving up things. You've got to give up on that particular issue if you want to get this project accepted." Compromise is a powerful force.

I learned about another powerful management tool in the Marine Corps during World War II. I was 17 when I enlisted, and I was called in right after my 18th birthday. Overseas I was an intelligence scout in the regimental headquarters company of the Ninth Marine Regiment. I was an intelligence scout, so I had more direct access to senior officers than the average enlisted man would. A mentor for me was the regimental commander—a colonel—a career marine corps officer who, by his example, was very inspiring to me. He would walk around and talk to people and be interested in what they were doing. I was surprised to learn that someone at that level of authority, particularly in the military structure, would be interested in what I was doing—an 18-year-old kid. He was a real inspiration to me. I've never forgotten that example. In the business world, it is a technique of business management known as MBWA—Management By Walking Around. Good managers manage that way. And good communities are run the same way.

It is very much like running a company. You have to have vision, to provide the leadership, or the stockholders will find somebody else who has it. When you're running a business, you should know exactly where the company ought to be five years from now and ten years from now. But you can't just jump from today to ten years ahead. You've got to work through every day to get there. There should be no mystery about where you want to be and what your business ought to look like. That should be true for a community as well.

One of the things that a chief executive officer does is set an example. In my experience, if the chief executive officer is a golfer, pretty soon, everybody in the company is playing golf. If the CEO is a tennis player, pretty soon, everybody's playing tennis. If the CEO is an amateur chef, pretty soon, everybody's having barbecues.

The people who have big stakes in the community have to get involved in the community. By setting examples, CEOs can encourage their employees to get involved. At one time, I was responsible for Transamerica's charitable foundation. When we got requests for donations from communities all around the country, the first question we'd ask was, "What's the extent of our own employees' involvement in this?" I think it's essential that the leaders—the people who have the business interests in the community—get involved beyond just their own business. Community involvement is an important example to set.

Most of the people who are moving to the valley are older. They're concerned about crime; they're interested in government; they're interested in culture. They're interested in preserving this valley. They're concerned about things that are going to impact unfavorably the quality of life that brought them here. That's the real challenge that this whole community faces now. How to keep from burying your head in the sand and saying, "No development." Because that is just not possible. You can't do it. But unless development is properly managed and controlled, there's going to be a whole bunch of tacky stuff created—the kind of development that has ruined so many other communities.

Only if the community is successful, economically and in other ways, can the community afford to support the educational system, to control crime, to do things for young people, and become the kind of community we want to see it become. People have asked me, "Why do you get involved in these things?" I have a simple answer: This is my home. And I want it to be a good place to live. I want it to be a successful community."

The Corporate Contribution

by Donald McComber

There is a major role for American business in assisting the community to develop. But—the role can only be filled by some corporations—not all, and it goes beyond sending money!

How do I know? I was employed by one that did, one that didn't, and one that had good intentions. In 1954, Industrial Indemnity Company employed me as a trainee. Twenty-seven years later, after serving this dynamic property and casualty insurance company, and holding responsibilities in nearly every function, including executive vice-president, I joined the parent company, Crum & Forster, as vice-chairman and chief insurance officer. The third company, where I served as president, was the Fireman's Fund Commercial Insurance Company. These three companies are examples of corporations that did (Industrial), that didn't (Crum & Forster), and that had good intentions (Fireman's Fund).

So what is this important role? As usual, it is easy to describe and difficult to perform. First, the CEO must establish a culture which embraces the concept that employees are more important than anything else. Yes, even more important than profits, or customers, or shareholders. The CEO at Industrial established this culture and then made sure that the mission, the strategy, and the organization were consistent with the culture. At Crum & Forster the culture was very different, and the CEO made sure it stayed that way. At the Fireman's Fund we were working on the culture when we sold the company!

So let me describe how community involvement was accomplished at Industrial.

It is naïve to believe that profits are unnecessary. However, to establish profit as a single objective is worthless. Why not—"air is important to breathing." Solid, profitable results are the product of outstanding employees. Good employees cannot be secured and retained unless the corporate environment is such that they are recognized as key to a successful corporate journey.

Second, the concept of "family," of community, within the corporation is necessary. "All for one and one for all" is corny but powerful. This helps to eliminate "turf building," secrets, hierarchical organization, and a "class" environment.

Third, in the above-described culture, the mentality does not come about just because the CEO says she wants it! It must be carefully thought out, continually practiced, and taught through an approach under which the employee understands and believes in the benefits. This must be part of the performance objectives and measurement of each employee.

Fourth, there are techniques that must be adopted by management to "prove" to employees that (a) this is serious, and (b) this philosophy extends beyond corporate boundaries to the *families* and *communities*.

What are examples of "techniques"? One of the most important is the inclusion of programs that allow the employee to expand his/her mind beyond the skills necessary to the employees' responsibility, or even beyond the company's business. These programs are of a cultural nature, apolitical, and can include seminars, libraries of non-industry books, sabbaticals, and study courses.

Other techniques include "communication training on communication." Cross-discipline sharing of ideas, as well as upward and downward discussion, keep the organization "alive" and dynamic, which fosters growth and profitability. What do you have if you do all this? First, you have a condition in which you allow individuals to develop, expand, contribute, and work toward being a "whole person." Second, you have a corporation that has a recognizable "business way of life" that allows it to acquire and retain above-average people. Third, you have a corporation which has the means to share with its people a set of values that apply not only to the workplace—but outside the workplace. The values and techniques that breed success "on the job" are "community" driven, and the same as those that are needed to succeed in family and community development.

The employee of today has many challenges. One of these is the division of time between job and family. HOW to use time, since there is only so much, is important. The contribution of the employer here is twofold:

(1) Allow the employee time for other than direct job activity.
(2) Assist the employee in identifying thought patterns and rhythms that lend to successes in all of his activities.

If the above is good for the employee relative to the job, and the family, then let's extend this one more time—to the community.

The average corporation, as a "good citizen," sends money to communities for apparent worthwhile causes. But who knows best what is worthwhile? And what is more important to the community than money? Time? And dedication? And understanding? And knowledge? Yes—and only individuals, collectively, can provide these essential elements. We gave them the opportunity at Industrial and it worked!

One need go no further than the Napa Valley, in Napa County, California, to observe what a community needs to have successes. The Agriculture Preserve legislation protected Napa for its future. Measure A legislation solved an age-old flooding problem. These are truly great success stories.

How did they happen? A group of people devoted time, possessed dedication, gained knowledge, and created understanding. The essential elements of a "community" activity were brought to bear on these two occasions, and there were more, which have made Napa a better place to live.

So how can large corporations use and be used by this new community vision? Think of a community where private people make the choices that govern their lives. Part of that is choosing businesses that will pay attention to community. Big corporations' senior officers forget that they are owned by people who live in communities all over the country. These shareholders can be boosters of company policy as members of their community. They can come to national shareholders' meetings and represent the views of their community. Also they can represent the corporations to the community in cultural language so that in the end the big, soulless corporation acquires a soul.

Now, let's go one step further. Let's use these same senior officers, once retired, to assist in working on effecting major improvements in the community. As an example, the Napa Valley is a community capable of working out many of its own health problems. The community is bigger than doctors and hospitals. The community must take responsibility for the health of its own members. Maybe an independent nonprofit center to speak for it? This could be made up of physicians, retired businesspeople, and other community members. Here is what a group like this could accomplish. Disease has multiple causes, therefore, concentrating on disease requires taking occasional photocopies of a person's life. A healthy person is less likely to become ill than is an unhealthy one. Each person should have a record of his or her health from birth—practices that have personally encouraged health and practices that have discouraged health. People living in strong, active communities are healthier than those who don't.

Physicians, hospitals, and business can be uniquely involved in the creation of community in the years ahead. There is a system in which each individual in the community would have an individual disk with his or her medical history on it. The doctors and hospitals would add to the individual's disk at each encounter. It would be up to each individual to provide information from birth. Thus it would be a current health biography. The community's central health center could help each person get their disk or other computer device started. Then it would be their responsibility to keep it up to date. The two systems could operate together or separately. Community means everyone is responsible.

One could send a doctor a report on a brain-tumor patient that would go way beyond the usual X-ray and accompanying analysis. The system would simultaneously attach relevant articles from the latest scientific journals, offering the doctor the most up-to-date medical data to help in planning treatment. The system would offer a built-in search engine to help the physician, creating a virtual university environment in which to practice medicine.

Medical care would be delivered almost entirely on an outpatient basis—hence a reduced need for beds. Medical information would be transmitted through computers and cyberspace—so old-fashioned charts would vanish.

Patients will be the caregivers, ministering to their own health needs, and turning only occasionally to doctors for advice or support. Doctors must be totally comfortable with the idea of recording and transmitting information into computers, and getting rid of inefficient paper charts, making it possible to maintain a patient's entire medical record digitally.

The hospital of the future has to speak two languages—the language of health and wellness and the language of healing, which is curing disease. Rather than continue the American trend of sending the elderly away—be it to retirement homes or nursing homes—why not try to keep them in the community, no matter what their age? Instead of treating seniors in a geriatric ward, use healing neighborhoods or sections of the hospital where people go depending on their disease, not their age. Don't keep people exiled, either at the end of life or at the early stages of life.

An innovation could be a call button on the bed that connects directly to the nurse, not the nursing station. Scenes common in modern hospitals are where patients ring and ring, begging for help. A patient in distress can reach out and summon an individual nurse, even when she is on a break!

We have classically defined hospitals as a place where sick people go. But if hospitals reinvent themselves as health systems, then it makes sense to build facilities that do a lot, but don't include as many hospital beds.

The cornerstone of most prevention efforts in the future will be gene discoveries. Already, several gene variations that raise the risk of major diseases have been discovered, including BRCA1 and BRCA2, which also drastically increase the odds of getting ovarian cancer, and APOE-4 for Alzheimer's disease.

Over the next ten years, advances in genetic testing will have a profound impact on medical care. Already, people are undergoing genetic testing for susceptibility to breast, colon, and ovarian cancer. And researchers are pushing ahead in their endeavors to discover genetic mutations that may predispose people to heart disease, other types of cancer, diabetes, and other illnesses.

The dynamism of the health care industry is probably the next challenge to many communities—certainly to the Napa Valley. The solution rests with the community. This means focusing the diverse talents of business, physicians, hospital administration, and others now so as to take full advantage of change.

The Wine Auction

by Robin Lail

I started working for Robert Mondavi as his executive assistant in 1977. What was so marvelous and life-changing about going to work for him is that my father was Robert Mondavi's mentor. Robert Mondavi was my mentor then, and he still is today. He is a man who definitely sees the glass as half-full. He has this wonderful attitude: "Do you realize how lucky you are?" "It's a great life if you don't weaken."

He overcame enormous adversities in his career, always turning problems into opportunities. When his family ousted him from Charles Krug Winery, he was 53 years old. This experience might have signaled the end of many people's active, creative careers, but not Bob Mondavi. He founded a brand new winery. And he set sail on a course which would prove to be brilliant. He has become the leading ambassador for wine in the world.

In 1979, he was invited by the St. Helena Hospital to chair a $6-million fund development campaign. He was so busy—he had just begun Opus One, a winery with Baron Phillipe Rothschild—and I knew the task would be extremely difficult. I urged him, "Don't do it. Don't do it." But he said, yes, he'd love to do it, and we were off to the races. We did all the things you normally do when you start a campaign like that. You first qualify your donors and you make lists and you check them and recheck them. We started calling on all the high-end potential donors first. As a result of one of those calls, a woman by the name of Pat Montandon came to the winery. She came with something she wanted, and, of course, we wanted something also, so it was one of those wonderful moments when two forces meet and something fantastic happens. Serendipity! She wanted to do an auction at her property, because she wanted to put on a large social event every year. People had been frowning on it, because a lot of people were left out. So, she decided that if she did something for the vintners then the party would not be frowned upon—it would be considered a good thing.

Margrit Mondavi immediately sat bolt upright in her chair and said, "But it's like the Hospices de Beaune. We can do this!" There is a wine auction in Burgundy for the Hospices de Beaune, which has been going on for over 200 years. It benefits the hospital in Beaune. And Bob said to me, "This is the event your father and I have been looking for all these years, to promote Napa Valley wines and to do a great thing for the community at the same time." Then, Bob and Margrit went on a trip. So it became my job to pull together this first auction.

In 1980, a group of us went over to the Hospice de Beaune to see exactly how that works. There were no models really. The Hospice was so different that we couldn't imitate it that much. All the wines are part of Clos de Vougeot. The wines are sold in the barrel. You'd better have a professional with you who's there as a buyer, because you must take the wines away with you after the auction. That sale usually establishes the price that Burgundian wines will sell for in that season. When you go to taste the wines, they're all in malolactic fermentation—it's in November. And you go down to the bastions of the Hospice du Beaune, and people are pouring wines from wine thieves into tiny silver taste de vins. The tasters are spitting the wines onto the gravel on the floor. And I arrived in an oyster-colored suit! It was a wonderful experience.

In 1981, the auction began. And I must say that it was quite fabulous. The people who built the first wine auction were my fabulous friends, my fabulous women friends. It took us two years to do it, but our steering committee did a brilliant job. Our auction—I can still feel the feeling in my stomach the day before the first gavel went down, because we truly didn't know what was going to happen. We didn't know if it was going to flop. We had 500 bidders—probably 250 bidders with their significant others. The event sold out, although it wasn't easy to sell it out. The auction was a fabulous success from the outset. That was one of the first things I ever remember putting into my personal bag of accomplishments, saying, "That was a good one."

The wine auction was a great thing. There were four goals for the auction. Our mission was to: (1) promote Napa Valley wines; (2) raise money for the local health-serving organizations; (3) promote good will between the vintners and the community, addressing The Queen of the Valley Hospital in Napa and the St. Helena Hospital. We started out benefiting just the two hospitals and expanded over time. And that happened also through the volunteer quotient. People take vacations to work on the auction. Last year, there were 1,400 volunteers working on the auction. This year they've cut back to 1,000.

And (4) we wanted to build a futures market for Napa Valley wines. That's why barrels were included in the auction. That was from the beginning. The first barrel tasting was at Meadowood, near where the swimming pool is. In the afternoon sun, it was probably 115 degrees. It was brutal. The wine wasn't boiling, but it was close to it!

There were a lot of people who wanted us to do the auction every other year, or every five years, to space it out, because it's a huge amount of work, and it's gotten bigger and more complex as time has gone on. We felt it was important to conduct the event every year so we would not lose our great momentum. It was the quintessential win-win situation. It was a marvelous opportunity to promote the Napa Valley appellation.

I sat in a vintners meeting this morning. There I was, looking around the room and seeing—there's Jack Stewart, and there's Jim Allen, and just delighting in seeing these people—I didn't know everybody in the room. Some I would call friends, some I would call different kinds, not as intense, friends. It was a wonderful sense of community. Nowhere else in the world do vintners act in concert the way they do here. There is enormous competition in the wine world. I want to have the most wonderful wine ever made on the planet, and so does everybody else I know that's making wine the way we are. And not everyone feels this sense of unity. Some people are very protective. They don't want their secrets to be shared, but by and large, this community of vintners and growers acts as a *community* of vintners and growers. We do things together, we promote things together. We travel together in large groups, and go around to promote the appellation, our pride in our beautiful appellation. If I'm in trouble, he'll help me. I know he will. And if he won't, she will. There's a buoyancy in that community.

We used to give a luncheon at Merryvale, which we patterned after an event at the Hospice de Beaune. After the auction every year, on Monday, they'd give a luncheon in Mersault. When you go to this luncheon, it is requested that you take a bottle of your favorite Burgundian producer's wine to this luncheon and the wines are shared. We used to do a luncheon for 100 people at Merryvale in the cask room. We would invite people to bring a bottle of their favorite wine produced by a Napa Valley vintner. They would walk in, and they would be very uncomfortable when they arrived at the winery. They would go into the cask room and tip their chairs forward, and put their bottle down in front of those chairs, and the devil take the hindmost if anyone thinks you're going to touch this thing. We would serve some wine before lunch, and then start lunch, and I would get up and make a speech about how we felt that this was a really glorious moment for Napa Valley, and that we were so glad that all these people had come to share in our great good fortune, and that our idea was to celebrate Napa Valley, not just the wine at Merryvale, but the wines of Napa Valley. We would hope that people would be so inclined to share the wines that they had brought along with them.

It was an Italian luncheon, catered by Tra Vigne. We had this wonderful music from creaky old guys who went by the name of the Godfathers, and they would come in their Italian costumes—their white shirts and green cummerbunds and red scarves and black pants, and they would play the accordion and mandolin and violin, and they were very jolly, and they'd play this wonderful Italian music. The waiters would bring in these enormous platters of food. Everything was family style. You cannot remain rigid in your chair if you want to eat, because you're going to have to help move the platters around the table. Slowly but surely, this aloofness would start to deteriorate and the noise level would start to rise. The luncheons were so great. The wines were shared with pleasure.

VII
The
Future
of
the
Community

Traditions

by Robin Lail

Our family tradition was started back in 1879 with my great-granduncle. Many traditions in the wine business—putting wine in bottles after it had been in barrels, a lot of planting techniques that today are being heralded as new and avant-garde—he was doing them before the turn of the century. My father inherited Inglenook. He always considered himself a conservator of Inglenook. Always for his children and his grandchildren.

The sense of community in the valley certainly went back to my father's generation. It was a very interesting society at that time. It was very stratified. The old families saw the old families socially. The new families coming into the valley—new, young families that started coming here in the 50s and 60s, pretty much saw the young families. This structure finally started to break down in the 60s, which was very good, I think. And in spite of the fact that the society was very stratified, at the same time, Napa Valley was already a marvelous community. The kind of community that I'm talking about—it is a vertical thing. To my father's funeral came such a wide variety of people. To my daughter's wedding came such a wide variety of people. People thought that the wedding was going to be a very social event—it was instead a very sociable event.

If something went awry, the community was there—all kinds of people—people who didn't have much, people who had a lot. And the community was already looking after the people who were looking after them, most specifically, the Hispanics who were here taking care of the vineyards and the walnut orchards. Was it universal? No. I don't think so. I don't think it's universal today. There is a fabulous strain of ore that runs through the strata of this valley, this incredible wealth of human beings.

I was a young woman who came from a "very nice family" who had Inglenook, the quintessential winery in the Napa Valley, and, by the way, a gorgeous property. I am not sure that I thought I was spoiled then, but now I suspect I was. My father had always told us, "This will all be yours one day." And then, my father died, and my mother sold the property. Suddenly, it was not mine. It took some time to recover from the shock of the loss.

In 1972, my husband Jon and I moved back to Napa Valley. I couldn't figure out what I was going to do for work. I couldn't see where I could fit. Then I started the Volunteer Center in Napa County.

The Volunteer Center was funded by a one-year, one-time $19,000 grant. One year. When I left, the Center had $500,000 in funding. We had started the transportation system that still runs around the community, enabling many elderly people to remain in their homes, providing them with a way to get from Point A to Point B, to see the doctor or get groceries. Running the Center was a wonderful experience, and really got me thinking a lot about community.

In 1981, Robert Mondavi introduced me to Christian Moueix, one of the most highly regarded winemakers in the world. Christian and I founded a venture called Dominus, and I started Merryvale with another group of partners. It was a wonderful time, and I learned a great deal about the wine business, but these businesses did not really satisfy my need to carry the family tradition forward to the fourth and fifth generations. When I looked at our two daughters, I knew there was no way I could pass that tradition along to them. It just wouldn't work. At the same time, I had never asked them if they wanted to have the business passed along to them, because I never wanted to force them into going into the wine business. I wanted them to walk through that door themselves with their own gusto and passion. Otherwise, there's no point in doing it. I'm a real believer in the maxim that we should pursue the things that are exciting to us and that we feel really good about. Where we think we can make a contribution.

In 1995, we bought a 20-acre property on Howell Mountain—I call it "the ranch." For us, it is "the ranch." It's astoundingly beautiful. And why? Well, it's not anything *we* did to this property. It's where the property is. It sits and looks out across the valley. It looks over the top of Kornell Rombauer, directly across the valley at Diamond

Mountain, the southern side. You can't see Mt. St. Helena, which is my favorite mountain, but when I'm coming down our mountain, I can see the top of it—it's kind of like an appetizer. And then our view goes all the way over to the coastal hills of Mendocino. It's a very private view. There's a big knoll that comes out to the right and a big knoll that comes out to the left and between these two beautiful knolls is this lovely pastoral view of this gorgeous place that changes every single day. This is the view I knew as a child—so pastoral.

We started this little business: Lail Vineyards. And before we started the business, I spoke with the girls—they were 23 and 25 at the time—and said, "We're looking at starting a new wine business. I've never asked you this question, but do you think you might have any interest in coming along at some point into the business?" And they both said, "Yes, we would." And then I said, "Of course, I understand you're 23 and 25, so you're not held to that, but it is just an expression of interest, and if it holds together for you, nothing could be more fabulous. And if it doesn't, nothing could be more fabulous. We want you to pursue your dreams." So we started.

I remember, because wine is so much a part of my life, that for many years I felt uncomfortable when people would talk on and on about their passion and the wine business. I thought it was a little overblown. I would talk that way, but I'm not sure my full emotional force was there with me. Now, all of a sudden, I found myself talking passionately about this business. So passionately! And my face would light up. And Jon loves being in it, and out in the vineyard that we have, on our ranch, walking through it every day. People talk about their vineyards being gardens. It's true. If it's not right, then you need to make it right, because it's a garden that you treasure. So, I'm completely immersed in this venture. It's meant to be a maximum 2,500-case operation, and right now we're in Year 4 and it's a 600-case operation. But we're building it.

Our youngest daughter, Shannon, is on the winery Board of Directors and is a great promoter of the brand. Our oldest daughter Erin is working as Operations Manager. It is difficult to describe what a joy it is to work with them. It is somehow very validating and exciting to have your children bring their new ideas and bright intelligence to your business. It is one of the most enriching experiences of my life.

I remember when Erin and I went to San Francisco to do our first tasting together. For the first half-hour, Erin was behind my left shoulder, and then she was right up alongside my left shoulder, pouring wine and chatting away with people. She was spectacular. We had six bottles of wine. The tasting was supposed to last five hours. We were out of wine in two hours, and it wasn't because I was there. No. It was because there was this wonderful energy standing right beside me. It was because the two of us were there. It was a great one–two punch. There's something so special about your child following a path that you embrace. It's not about ego. It's just pure delight.

After the Immigrants

by Rich Salvestrin

My grandparents immigrated from Italy. They had friends and felt welcome here. In 1932, they were able to purchase a small piece of land on the south end of St. Helena. That's where we've been ever since. My father was born and raised on the property. He grew up working vineyards with my grandfather. I was born there as well, so I'm third generation. It's been a blessed place to grow up. The community here is so small, and people care so much that everybody looks out for each other.

For my grandparents, it was very close knit here, very ethnic—an Italian crowd that they socialized with. Sons of Italy. Italian-Catholic Federation. I certainly recognized a generational difference in the social community from my grandparents to my parents to my generation, but what hasn't changed is the focus on family and being an active part of the community. Life in a small community like we have means pitching in and doing your part to help make it a better place.

I grew up in the vineyard. When I was growing up, I was less interested in grape growing, just because as a kid, I was playing sports, and all those other things were going on in high school. But by the time we could hold a pruning shear in our hands, we were trimming the vines in front of my dad and my grandfather, so they wouldn't have the brush to handle. We also did a lot of shovel work. We grew up doing it, so it was second nature to us. Before I even got out of high school, I knew I was going to study viticulture, because I wanted to come back here.

After school, my brother and I would walk over to my grandparents' house. They had a very big influence on our life. We would sit and listen to stories about what happened in Italy, what happened here, and what the differences were. They were amazing stories. Many people leave their home and start a new life somewhere else, but at that time it was quite a risk. If I think of myself in that situation it really puts it into perspective.

My grandmother was very good at making you aware of how important family was. I'll never forget: when I was very, very small, she said to me, "Your name is all you have." They worked very hard to have a piece of land and a home. They weren't wealthy, but they were very well respected in the community. She said, "We worked hard to be accepted here in a country that we're not from. Your name is who you are. It's your integrity. You should never do anything to spoil that." That was ingrained in us from an early age.

When I got out of college, I was anxious to get to work. I had a goal to build on what my grandfather started and to one day bring our family vineyard operation full circle by putting our name on the bottle of what would be the best expression of our site. We are now in our third vintage. During our replanting process, a property that adjoins my parents' ranch became available. I was very familiar with this property because during my high school years the neighbor hired me to do tractor work for him. Having that relationship allowed me the opportunity to lease and eventually purchase that piece of property. For me, owning a piece of land or vineyard meant achieving a goal. It is truly a feeling of pride and accomplishment to work your own land.

I can have a religious experience every day, just by being part of this valley. It's incredible. Sometimes, it's being on a tractor, sulfur dusting at six o'clock in the morning as the sun comes up. To see the way the sun is coming up over the hills, the way the clouds are gathering, and the moon is going down on the other side, and the stars are still there. Sometimes, you just have to stop and look at it. Appreciate it. It can happen every day, especially here. The way the sun hits a vineyard in the afternoon. It puts a certain hue on the whole landscape. It's incredible. It doesn't matter where you are in the valley. It's all what you make it.

The Farm Bureau has a group called Young Farmers and Ranchers, designed to bring young people into the group, to familiarize them with the organization. You socialize a little bit, meet other people in your age group, and have the opportunity to participate in leadership conferences at the state level. I was invited to have a steak and a beer with the local group and was drawn in. It was good for me because I learned a tremendous amount. You may have had a challenge come up in your vineyard, and somebody might have had that same problem two years ago. They'll say, "This is what we did." It was social, but a lot of it was just getting together and seeing what was going on in the industry. It was good networking. The programs offered at the state level, I thought, were an excellent learning experience and an opportunity to learn about the Farm Bureau and develop leadership skills.

The basic philosophy of the Farm Bureau is that it unifies the growers in the valley to give us the opportunity to work cooperatively and protect the agricultural heritage we have here. We need to be proactively involved in shaping policy that affects our industry.

On the other hand, as farmers, we need to listen and work with the community and try to be good neighbors. We have to preserve this industry, but in the long run, preserving the industry means being a good neighbor and getting along with everyone. We have to do the right thing.

I like to compare the valley to a vineyard site: you have a certain soil you're dealing with, a certain microclimate, certain water availability. The spacing of your vines and design of your trellis system is dependent on these factors. Maximum quality is achieved at a certain yield level. That's the balance. That's the way I feel about this valley. There's an optimum balance of vineyards, people, natural environment, habitat—all those things. What we need to do is find that balance.

Wine and Art

by Mark Aubert

My parents moved here in 1970, when I was about 11 years old.
They wanted to get away from Sacramento because of crime and the
huge influx of people to the area where we were living at that time.
It was also to pursue the rural lifestyle and even more to pursue the
love of wine. My father loved wine. He learned it from his father,
and I learned it from my father—the love of agriculture and the love
of winemaking. They had a drugstore, but also developed a vineyard
and a wine lifestyle.

Of course, being young and easily influenced by agriculture,
I fell in love with it as well. Young boys always like tractors and
trucks and cows and horses. Here, it all came to reality. My fondest
memories are of growing up among the vines.

In 1976, I was working at a little winery called Rutherford Hill,
and I was also involved with Boy Scouts. The Scoutmaster was a
winemaker. Half the kids in the troop were involved in the wine business. It was Boy Scout/Wine Scout. The Scoutmaster was an incredible
man named Phil Baxter, who had a huge impact on me. He was very
dedicated and a good leader. Like a second father, he always tried to
get me to do better and better.

He taught me how to make wine. He liked my enthusiasm, so
he offered me summer positions at Rutherford Hill, to apprentice to
him. This went on for four summers, all through high school. Even
after I went off to college, he hired me back as an apprentice in the
summer. I had a huge leg up on all my classmates from Fresno, because
a lot of these kids had never even worked in a winery. Growing up
here was very important.

My parents wanted me to become an engineer. When I graduated from high school, it was the boom time of Silicon Valley and the wine industry was in a recession. So they tried to steer me toward engineering, but I fought that bitterly, because I wanted to live here. Some children want to leave the agricultural areas for the big cities. I guess if you don't like tractors, agriculture, and winemaking, what is there to do in Napa Valley?

I looked to the luxury wines, the very, very collectible—$50 and above. I aligned myself with people that I could learn a great deal from, so that I could create these very rare works of art. I've tried to exploit grape growing and winemaking to create an art form, like a painting or sculpture—so you work really hard to preserve that, and preserve this beautiful area. Something that is as rare and collectible as wine is—it cascades down to where the grapes are grown, the community, and the people involved. I've developed a lot of hype and fanfare for the wines I make. That's what I think this area needs.

I say that winemaking is 75 percent artistry and 25 percent science. I've chosen the route of artistry and the collectibility factor, instead of the technical, scientific side of winemaking. The greatest wines that come from Bordeaux are the artistic statements of the area. The winemakers and chateau owners use lots of adjectives and talk about the seasons and the soil and the sun and the moon and the stars. That's artistry. To put that into the wine's taste is artistry. The science filters in as reinforcement. Wines are very complicated chemical things. You need to have a lot of science background to know what's going on, but the consumer wants to hear about the artistry, how you portray and describe to others the techniques that we use.

You can paint with oils or watercolors—well, my paint is grape flavors. We try to nurture these vineyards to produce certain flavors. For instance, we talk about the grapes having a certain level of concentrated fruit flavors. I try to portray that in my dialogue to people. It's hard for you to understand, if you're not a huge wine afficionado, what I'm talking about if I say the wines smell like earth and boysenberry flavors and they have a near-term drinkability and all these things. The artistry is to describe that to people, to describe my artwork verbally.

We're not talking about large case production. We're talking about single-vineyard designations, fundamentally, great vineyards that have great earth—just like Mouton—that can stand alone as single-vineyard bottlings. If I take a property, it has to stand alone as a vineyard. We take twenty different lots of wine and blend them into one wine, and figure out whether it will age for twenty years or five years. And I do it with my taste buds. The human palate is more accurate than any machine. You can pick up nuances. My palate is very tuned.

As an artist, you pick up certain senses—blending is the true art form of winemaking. You don't want them homogeneous. You want some diverse ingredients in the flavor profiles. That's the magic about wine. You can take something as small as five acres and see five different things come out of it.

You nurture the wines when they are very young—just after they've finished fermenting—you're even talking to them when they're on the vine. As the wines get older, you listen to them. You're listening, but you're doing a lot of influencing, to get these flavors. You start when the grapes turn color. But upstream from all these things, you look at the vigor, the demeanor of the vine. The best vines are less vigorous and produce smaller crops. Vines that are more vigorous produce larger crops. You can actually look at a vine and have an intuition that these vines are going to make great wine, based on their demeanor. You can tell if they're going to make poor wine, based on their demeanor. Demeanor is the vine's attitude toward where it's living. You're giving this little plant a space to live in. Is it happy living in that space? You're talking about a 3-foot by 5-foot or 3-foot by 7-foot space. It puts its roots down there. It grows its leaves. Is it happy living there? Is it sad? Is it overly anxious? It's how they like it or don't like it. That influences the wine incredibly. It's a direct result. A little bit of stress is good, to some people. I believe that vines should be content living in their space.

That's part of the artistry, too. There are older vines, for instance, wiser vines, or young, nervous vines. You develop a rapport. You have to create your own hype and excitement. That's what I love doing more than anything.

As I became an artist, I chose the French, *terroir* model, which is what the earth and the sun and the rocks give to the grape and give to the wine. I have a lot of science verbiage that I use from time to time, but the consumer I've chosen to align myself with likes to hear the collectibility factor and the great soil types, the neighborhood. A rocky soil should produce wines with terroir. We know the wine will have a mineral quality to it, if we do the winemaking correctly. If the vines like living in that space, they're going to pick it up.

I'm looking for complexity, balance, seamlessness—so that the flavors are integrated from start to finish. Ageability is very important too. I want the wines to be on a curve so that they increasingly get more complex as the years go on. Cabernet needs to get silkier, softer as the years go on, more hedonistic. Hedonism in wine is a very important quality in a rare and collectible wine. The consumer wants to feel the enthusiasm I put into that bottle of wine. My wines are very hedonistic—they're full of richness and flavor.

Color and clarity are almost a given. Wines need to be clear, they need to be finished properly. They need to be aseptic. You don't want them to spoil in the bottle. Wine is a great hygienic beverage—clarity is just so basic I don't even talk about it.

People are still trying to preserve and enhance the area viticulturally. These are very successful individuals—they truly want to create wines that are world class. A lot of people have second homes. Do they have deep roots here? Probably not. Are they concerned about local issues? Probably not. Do they build a rapport with their neighbors? Probably not. That's something to grapple with. There are a lot of absentee owners coming in here who are changing the local flavor. When you grow up here and you see the seasons change, and you grow older with people, you are more interested in what they're doing, but if you come here six months a year, or once a week, or jet in once a month, it's very different.

A lot of my friends are living the same sort of dream. They're trying to better themselves, better the community. That's one thing I'm lacking—I'm not giving back to the community. But I'm still young. I need to get some of these transitional things in my career done, and then I'll start giving back to the community—volunteering. I've taken a lot and I want to give back. A lot of my friends feel the same way—through nonprofit, through donations. One thing I do—I donate a lot of the wines I make to charitable causes. They generate a lot of money for local charities.

Stewards of the Soil

by Andrew Hoxsey

Someone once said, "The best fertilizer you can give to
your vines is footprints." —Andrew Hoxsey

I'm fourth generation here. My grandfather, Andrew Pellisa, was
born in 1906 in Calistoga. He was a grape grower and managed the
family vineyard up there. His father died when he was in his early teens.
He claims he was the first man ever to irrigate a vineyard in Napa
Valley. He was right on a little creek there that ran into the Napa River,
and he was able to divert the creek. So, it goes way, way back.

My grandfather,was a Planning Commissioner for almost 18 years.
He has been given a lot of the credit for the Ag Preserve. It was the germ
of an idea that he had, and he mentioned it to somebody, and it came
back in a different iteration. He used to say, with some regularity, that
nobody ever owns the soil. We're all stewards of the soil. End of conversation. So, we want to pass the soil on to the next generation in better
shape than the previous generation found it. This is something that he
did. I think he had a kind of Midas touch: everything he did with the
soil—whether he had his hands in it or not, he seemed to get good
crops—his timing was always good. Maybe it's luck, maybe it's not. He'd
find himself in a situation, and the land always seemed to bail him out.

As a baby, his mother would put him into a grape box to take a
nap as she was working in the field. And his father died, so he had to
take care of this damn vineyard, so he didn't have real good memories
of vineyards. When he actually left the farm and came down all of
15–16 miles to the Yountville area, he started a dairy farm, but he
always wanted to be a cowboy. That was his life's ambition. He liked
beef cows, and that whole romance.

I look at myself as a little different. I still consider myself a farmer, but more importantly, I consider myself a businessman/entrepreneur. I think, to carry on his legacy, you can have the same compassion, but you have to monitor the bottom line. With the value of the underlying real estate—you hate to think about it—my grandfather in those days had the right and ability, because he owned it all, to say, "I don't care about return on investment. I don't care about this. I'm doing what I want to do. End of conversation." At this point in time, there are more owners than just my grandfather, although they are basically family members. I feel that to keep his memory alive, I have to keep the property whole, and to keep the property whole, I have to generate a return on investment, certainly better than if they sold it all and put it in CDs. And that's tough to do, with the underlying value of the real estate.

Our labor rates are about a third higher than in the Central Valley. Housing in this valley is tremendously expensive, and I don't know what to do about that, other than build homes. We typically provide more benefits to our workers. These things are wonderful and they are a part of our community. I think we should be proud that labor is more expensive, because we have been able to give people a better lifestyle. As long as we can afford it, we should do it. But there's a farmer in the Central Valley saying, "It's not sustainable. I can't afford it. I get one-tenth of what Andy Hoxsey gets for his grapes." So labor is your biggest issue.

Then there's the dust issue. Let's say that a government body says, "We're going to reduce dust by 50 percent." So somebody raises his hand in the back and says, "That's easy. Plant a permanent cover crop." At face value, that sounds like a real, real good idea. Let's plant. But then, as a farmer, you have to step back and realize that for every action that I do, there's an equal but opposite reaction. So, what problem is coming down the road at me because of a permanent cover crop? It may be a frost issue. Soil is about a degree and a half warmer. By viticultural practices, you can affect your microclimate by about three degrees. If you chop the grass very low—that will warm it a degree and a half. If you disk the grass under, you increase the temperature another degree and a half. With wind machines, maybe you can get another degree, and smudge pots—probably not quite a degree. Smudge pots are probably your last choice—let's see—"return stack orchard heaters" is the politically correct term. So, in the whole scheme of things, being able to disk under your permanent cover is one of the most important things we can do for frost protection. And even if you can solve that problem, you probably have a mole or vole problem coming your way, where they eat the roots of the vines.

When I make a decision, I look at a whole bunch of issues, not just "does it make dust?" This is the whole thing about organic farming: it's a grand circle. Everything that you do has an effect on something else. So, what you're trying to do is maintain some sort of a balance so that the bad critters are minimal. We've got this one bug called a thrip that in the early part of the year, if it's rainy and cool, he's a bad guy. You can get stunting. But once the vine gets out about 12 inches, he now becomes a beneficial. What if, during that period that he's a bad guy, you did something about it, and now you've lost your beneficial? Things have a way of working themselves out.

We've got this malady called Pierce's Disease in the valley. I've got a huge problem with it. I'm on the river and the hill, which are the two sources of it. I think you've got to stand back and say that the fact that you have the problem is a symptom of a bigger problem. You'd better figure that out before you start nuking that poor little bug.

I have a real concern that in some ways we've forgotten our roots in this valley. As farmers. I know it's still the Ag Preserve, but from my perspective, we're trying to turn Napa Valley into a postcard, where you can take a picture, but nothing else ever happens. It's just that picture, the way you see it. Farming is not like that. It's ever-changing. People scream about dust. With the frost last year—which we haven't had in many, many years, a heavy frost season—in the Coombsville area one night they were starting wind machines, and they got 80-some-odd 911 calls.

Napa Valley is paradise on earth. There are no ifs, ands, or buts about it. And I believe there is a cost to living in paradise. We're treading dangerously close to a time when outside influences—government—might increase the cost of making wine to the point where the consumer is not going to pay the ten times more for Napa Valley wines. Right now, I would say that the chances are pretty slim that we can compete in the world market for our products because of the underlying cost of doing business. Or because of the lifestyle, it will be very chic to own vineyards with no hope of ever making a cent out of them.

If you have people that care about what they're doing and are concerned about their community and the environment, those people are probably going to pass the ground on in better shape than it was in when they received it. I don't know how you test whether people have that passion. In some ways, the Ag Preserve is us protecting us from ourselves.

Going into the Vineyard

by Beth Novak Milliken

I was 11 when we moved here. It was a lifestyle change for my parents. My dad was a doctor and wanted to be a farmer. We bought a beautiful property, although at that age I didn't realize it, and we started growing grapes.

I'll never forget the big dinner-table talk after we moved up here. I was 11 or 12. We were in the dining room, and dad said, "You kids have lived too high on the hog for too long. Things are going to change." What changed was that we had to go out into the vineyard every summer. Dad wasn't going to let us lounge around. We had to go out and work for four hours every morning, Monday to Friday, in the summertime. It was really, really good. And then we got all afternoon to play—to swim, skateboard, bike ride. They paid us—not much—but we were paid so we could have money in our pockets. We earned what we got, and we still do. Granted, we come from a very fortunate background, but we weren't just handed things on a platter. We learned to have an appreciation for what we have. Appreciation of the land goes along with that too.

My dad had a heart attack and died after we had been here four years. He was 44. That was not easy to get through. I was 16, a sophomore in high school, and I was thinking, "I'm going to be a doctor." When I went off to college in 1979, I went to UCLA because I wanted to go to a school where one class was as large as my whole high school.

If it wasn't for mom being as strong as she was after dad's death, I don't know what we would have done. She's incredibly strong. She's an example for me. She said, "I have five children, I've got a vineyard. I've got to keep it together and make this work."

Mom had never been in the business world. After dad died, she had to go to Mike Robins, who owned Spring Mountain at the time, and say, "Do you want to buy my grapes?" She would look at the ground as she said this. She didn't know what she was doing. It was all new to her. And the industry was a lot more male-dominated then, so she was selling grapes to men, but she didn't ever feel any resistance. She started selling her grapes, and people—especially John Shafer and the Duckhorns—would tell her, "You know, your grapes are really good. You should consider doing something with them." So dad's dream became her dream, too.

I graduated from UCLA, moved to San Francisco, and got into the wine industry. I was selling wine for a broker—selling a lot of Napa wines, as it turned out. The only reason I got the job is because I had lived in the Napa Valley. I had worked at Sterling as a tram girl one summer and cleaned up the lawns at Mondavi after concerts one summer, so it wasn't as if my wine knowledge was vast, but I had the interest, and it was fun.

While I was working in the city, my mom gave me a call one day and said, "You know, I could use a little bit of help up here. Maybe you'd want to come up a few days a week." I said, "Sure. I'll do that." So I start driving up a couple days a week in 1987. We had an ongoing wine business then and mom didn't want to do the day-to-day work. She's great at it, but that's not what she likes to do. My part-time job quickly turned into a full-time responsibility. John and I got married in early 1988 and moved up here. I was worried about John moving to the Napa Valley. He's from Chicago originally, and I wondered if he'd like the valley and St. Helena. I thought it might be too small for him. But he loves it up here. He's very community-minded, and we have gotten more and more involved as time has allowed. Those first years, when you start any new job you're just working nonstop, trying to figure it all out; so I was working all the time trying to get everything together.

I'm thankful that I never felt any pressure to come back to the Napa Valley. It wasn't like, "Hey, there's this family business and we expect you or your siblings to come back." It was always open-ended. I hope I will be the same way with my children. Just because you have a family business, it doesn't mean that someone in the family should be in it, unless they have the aptitude and they're truly interested.

Once a month we have a group meeting at Spottswoode to discuss a philosophical topic. Today our topic was, what do you find sustaining about your job? I think what's really nice about our business is the real collaborative nature of our work. I have the title of president and Diane Armstrong is vice-president and my sister Lindy manages our sales. We also have two other female employees—our winemaker, Rosemary Cakebread, and Paige Peterson, who assists in all aspects of sales, marketing, and administration. We really run a democratic company. Everybody is very involved. We work very collaboratively. For our newsletter, one person may start a lead article, then we all sit down and work on it so that, ultimately, it comes from a common voice. We really share in the decisions.

Before returning to Spottswoode, I was in wine sales. There were more men in wine sales than women, but I never felt remotely unwelcome. It didn't affect me when I was president of the Napa Valley Vintners Association in 1988—yes, I was the first female in its 50-year history. It's been an old boys' network up here, and to a certain degree it still is, but it really isn't a big deal. I didn't want the press release to say, "She's the first woman." I didn't think it needed publicizing. If you do a good job, it really doesn't matter if you're male or female. You just need to do your job well, with intelligence, humor, and grace—whether one is male or female is a nonissue.

Futures

by Jim Gamble, Hugh Davies, and Tom Gamble

Hugh Davies;

"Growing up in the Napa Valley was a tremendous experience. It's an extraordinary place, a place I feel very tied to. I went away to high school, where some students didn't have the same bond to home that I felt. More strikingly, that was true when I went to college. It would have been very hard not to go home, not to continue to live in this place that I felt so close to. So I came back when I was 22.

"I wasn't sure exactly what I wanted to do, but I was drawn back home. I can't imagine having grown up in a better place, and that can only be true for another generation if this place is preserved. I started realizing that our way of life in this community doesn't exist by chance."

Tom Gamble;

"After a year of work on the Farm Bureau Board, I see that a generational shift in attitudes and perceptions of what Napa County is and what it should be is underway. Agriculture in Napa County is perceived as successful and in many ways it is. But the displays of wealth that the tourist-oriented portion of the wine industry displays upsets many voters in Napa County's two most important cities, Napa City and American Canyon, because they see themselves as having been ignored and left out of the good times while the wine guys get rich. A debate in itself, but the have/have-not feeling is really there. It has started to change, but for the most part, we have ignored our city neighbors while we flourished and their downtowns decayed.

"Over the last thirty years, preserving agriculture meant making hard decisions, limiting land-use choices in favor of agriculture, accepting short-term unpopularity and ingratitude for those actions, and accepting less than the total, maximum return possible on one's land, since we give up the right to develop for the right to grow grapes. But in return we have fewer competing uses in the wine-growing zones, thus giving us a chance to keep agriculture. The debate is not the same as it was thirty years ago. The debate question being thrust upon us today by the general populace is not protecting the wine industry, but asking what the limits of it are going to be. We are now in a period of change where the agricultural community and the community at large are asking themselves, should we continue the sacrifices previous generations have made to keep agriculture going?

"Further, the majority of Napa County's voting population no longer works directly in agriculture, so the population is losing touch with what the needs of a viable wine industry are. If that's the reality, what does it mean? It means urban voters don't necessarily have the same way of looking at rural land use as the wine industry does. It means that agriculture in Napa County is no longer the sole political superpower in the county. It means that newcomers and even born-and-raised town kids don't understand why they should put up with the inconveniences of living next door to farms. Wind machines with their airplane-sized engines coming on at 2:00 A.M. to protect the vines from frost, or Bed and Breakfast guests filing complaints about predawn tractoring."

Hugh Davies;

"Along those lines, in 1988, Tom and Jim Gamble, Derek Dwyer, Beth Novak, Kasia Winiarski, Bill Davies, and I—encouraged by our parents—put together a group called the Napa Agricultural Preservation Association. There must have been six or eight meetings, maybe even more. It was designed to educate ourselves and try to encourage other young people to learn a bit more about how the county government had established the Ag Preserve, the zonings, the general plan, and other factors that allowed for all these good things not only to be as they were then, but also to maintain them in the future.

"A shift of power took place. Our parents were very powerful people. They told us to exercise our political muscles. They basically said, "This is your valley. This is your home. This is your place. This is going to be yours. If you guys want to keep it like it's been, then you better start getting on the ball. It's time to get to work." The

2020 issue, to preserve agricultural zoning in the valley to the year 2020, was an issue that we got behind. We sent out newsletters to educate the public about the initiative.

"We also did a fundraiser for Mel Varrelman, the supervisor for District 3, which is the north part of the valley—basically Calistoga, St. Helena, Angwin, Yountville. Mel was a school teacher in the 70s. When I was in first grade, he was the math teacher who came to school with an abacus. And then I had him as a teacher in junior high school. He's a good guy."

Jim Gamble;

"I remember Mel very well from those years. In the late 1980s, I was living in the San Francisco area and a group of friends from St. Helena, all in their twenties, were committed to the reelection campaign of Mel Varrelman, as Napa County Supervisor in the district representing the northern Napa Valley. Hugh and Bill Davies were involved. Tom Gamble and myself. Kasia Winiarski. Peter Kornell. Beth Novak Milliken. At the time, Jack and Jamie Davies, mom, the Winiarskis, and others were encouraging the young generation to get involved. They would say, "It's time to pass the reigns. We've done the Ag Preserve. We need new blood. We need new energy, new enthusiasm to carry this on, and so at that point in time, there was a bunch of us (i.e., the younger generation) living in or near the valley. Mel was in a tightly contested supervisor's race against a guy with a development agenda. His development objectives were very inconsistent with our stewardship ethics. So we got involved with Mel's campaign. Fortunately, Mel won by a landslide."

Hugh Davies;

"I have very strong hopes that things will remain intact in terms of the wine community, open spaces, natural beauty, and the strength of the watershed. I'm on the county's watershed task force now. The watershed task force is working to balance the community's economic and environmental goals.

"It takes 3¹/₂ hours every other Monday, and I work to prepare for those meetings. There are issues where consensus won't be reached, but we will produce solid recommendations for the county to move forward with. And I'm totally focused in my work here at Schramsberg. I wish that I could spend more time helping to preserve the valley. But I also realize that I wouldn't have the opportunity to do that if I didn't have this winery as well. There are other ways to make money, and maybe work less hard, but that's part of the program too. It is a balancing act."

Tom Gamble;

"There seems to be an unwillingness on the part of the cities of Napa County to increase their housing densities, zone for low-income and farm-worker housing, limit their use of groundwater, and forego expanding their city limits. This is not an issue-free relationship. And each one of these issues has the potential to keep a new generation of lawyers fully employed if we can't hammer out community consensuses as we did with the river. The rules are going to get changed because government is stepping in since the effort at self-regulation is failing and the general population is demanding change.

"My proposal? Its pretty simple. If we in the industry can reach an understanding, maybe we can more effectively reach out to the residents in town and the new urban refugees and engage in dialogue. We will probably find we have the same ultimate goals, Cabernet makes a better neighbor than condos. But perhaps we can also agree to travel the same path to reach that goal. We should be able to. The previous generation took a backwater industry and turned it into a world-class affair by talking. Have you ever heard Robert Mondavi talk? There was also yelling and swearing, but at least people kept cooling off and coming back to the table to hammer out cooperative solutions. While we were selling the world, we just forgot about our next-door neighbors. We should be able to fix that. If we can't now, while prices are good, how are we going to hang on when this cyclical wine industry takes its next down-swing?"

Jim Gamble;

"And that is exactly why Stephanie and I were interested in moving back to the Napa area. Even though the problems seem daunting at times, this community always pulls together and find solutions that make sense for everyone. In addition, we were interested in returning from Orange County because of our values, which are primarily focused on family, nature, and community.

"At the point in time that we made the decision to move back north, Sarah was nearly three years old and David was just an infant. I started reflecting a little bit on my childhood and my experiences and how that really helped form the person that I am, in terms of character, responsibility, discipline, all those things. I started thinking about Sarah and the experiences she was having. For example, we'd go to friends' houses, and they'd say, "Hi. Come on in. We're watching Scooby Dooby Doo with the kids. Would you like some popcorn?" Many of our friends, who we love dearly, literally parked their children in front of the TV for hours on end every day. That is when I realized we needed to get out of there. When I was growing up it was, "You kids, go outside and play. It's a beautiful day. Go find something to do, and by the way, I'm locking the doors behind you, so don't even think about getting back in the house for the next hour or two." Fortunately, our community was safe enough to be able to do that, but . . . that was the type of mentality I grew up with, and it wasn't until I was a bit older that I was able to understand how beneficial that philosophy was in terms of stimulating my mind and my creativity. In addition, spending so much time outside as a child, I really developed an appreciation for nature, and the delicate web in which we live, in terms of balancing the needs of a free market economy with those of the environment.

"One of the things I really appreciate about my upbringing was the stewardship ethic that my parents always exemplified, and which I unknowingly witnessed. Back when I was growing up on a good-sized, working cattle ranch in Oakville, the valley had lots of cattle, orchards, and vineyards. The wine industry was not the dominant industry that it is today. The wine industry was much smaller in the 60s and 70s. We spent a lot of time on the land. We became part of the land—working with our parents out on the land. Every morning we would get up at five, eat a scrambled egg breakfast, get on the tractor and hay wagon to go feed the cattle and manually move the irrigation pipe. By 6:30 A.M. we were back at the house to wash up and then ride our bike a mile down the end of the road to catch the school bus for a 45-minute ride in to school. That type of work ethic and that type of connection to the land becomes a part of you. When you live on the land, and enjoy the land, and see how beautiful the land is, you realize how preciously valuable that land is. When I was in southern California, there really was no stewardship of the land. In my view, economic return from the land was the primary focus.

"The values of many people here in the Napa Valley are very different than those in many other parts of the world. Here we value open space and are willing to fight tooth and nail to maintain that open space. Even though we are not maximizing the potential economic return of the land, we are preserving what I believe to be a national treasure, which the Napa Valley is, and placing a higher value on nature, on agriculture, on open space, and on community. And . . . we are looking for ways to grow our businesses without exploiting our natural resources.

"Stephanie and I both wanted our children to live in a community that had similar values, and so we decided to plant ourselves here in the Napa Valley. We might not have the best career opportunities, but we are awfully excited to be here, especially for the sake of our children."

Hugh Davies;

"I am very comfortable with the notion of living here for the rest of my life and working to build and preserve at the same time. To a certain extent, I very much feel like I'm on a mission. I think the key is the community-building that needs to occur right now. We need to continue to keep the agriculturalists and the environmentalists on the same side. That's critical. We need trust. We need to sit everybody down in a room . . ."

Jim Gamble;

"Through hard work by a lot of people, we will find solutions. And will have the chance to share with our children what we experienced while growing up here. Especially in terms of open space, of family, and of a tight-knit community. I would like to share with them the openness, green fields, the fields of mustard. Playing hide-and-seek in the mustard. Running around with the dogs. Playing with friends. Having space to ride horses and ride motorcycles and ride bicycles and play baseball. All that open space. And to go up to Berryessa Valley and enjoy the open space. The natural wildlife. The flora and fauna. The bald eagles and how they almost disappeared here in Napa Valley, and how, through a conservation program, are slowly returning. How beautiful that is. And also share with them a vision of what the land could look like through sound ranching and farming practices. We're starting to become more sensitive to the environmental issues. We're starting to put back into the land, and put back into the soil. I want to visualize with them what it could look like. The Berryessa Valley might become a huge wildlife preserve. Of how a privately operated cattle-ranching operation can coexist within that wildlife preserve, by working and cooperating with numerous governmental organizations to make it work. If I can share all of these things with my children, I feel they will have a tremendous foundation for living happy and fulfilling lives."

VIII
A
New
Vision
of
Community

A Collection of Thoughts
about Community

Sports can bring us together. If you go to a soccer game on Saturday, you're going to see the bank president standing next to the guy that picks up your garbage. You're cheering your kids, who are on the same team. That's true in any community. And there's a lot of involvement here, in the Little League and the soccer leagues. Sports do bring people together.

—Brian Kelly

A community is like a marriage—if you don't keep working at it, it either goes up or down. It doesn't sit still. You have to work on it.

—Brian Kelly

A thriving community has lots of diversity and lots of culture. Ethnic diversity and culture in an environment where everyone is accepting one another. That's part of the problem with our schools— people are intolerant of difference. I want my daughter to have a sense of self that is so strong that it can't be beaten down. I want her to love what's different. In the environment, diversity is important. People need to be surrounded by a spectrum of other people—lower income, middle income, high income. I think it's a crime that our school teachers can't live here, that they have to commute such long distances. And there should be cities, and there should be country. Let's isolate the urban areas and let the country be the country.

—Aimee Price

There are different qualities to the different energies. There are meridian lines similar to the ones that the Chinese see in our bodies and they can be activated to heal the earth. I just try to do that every step. That's what I wish to do—to listen more and be sensitive to what the earth needs. I do that with my garden. I watch what likes to grow there. You don't have to be a magical person to notice your surroundings. I was raised looking at books. I didn't have a lot of hands-on learning experiences. But if you just *look*, it's obvious. My garden likes to grow borage and callendula. Those are wonderful medicines. They're good medicines for me. One of my herb teachers once told me that whatever you need for your health is usually growing within a hundred feet of your front door. Look! Ask!

—Carolyn Sanders

People pulling together—that's really what community means. If you have a fire, everybody goes out and helps. Somebody's in trouble, and everybody goes out and helps. You argue with each other, just like any family, but nevertheless, they're all there to help each other out. We adopted our daughter in 1984. An adoption is always a risky deal, so we didn't buy anything. We picked her up at the hospital, went to Mervyn's and bought a blanket to wrap her in, and brought her home. When we got home, the kitchen was filled with stuff for her. Stuff kept showing up for weeks. A bassinet that was loaned to us. Stuff kept showing up. Everybody seemed to know that we adopted this girl.

—Mel Varrelman

Community

by Ken Norwood

The relationships which make a great community could exist in the country or in the city. Cherish them wherever they occur. In the beginning, humans extracted and used resources from the earth to sustain themselves and their village settlements around the continents. These earliest people, and most people up until very recently, lived in harmony with their ecosystems, relatively aware of the limits of their geographic and climactic environs, extracting only what was needed for their sustenance. They developed a social and environmental relationship with the land and resources that was reflected in their extended family, tribal, and village social order.

Over time villages grew into towns and cities, but for tens of thousands of years the expenditure of energy was practically all human and animal. Cities evolved around the human scale of transportation, walking and riding on common conveyances: wagons, trains, and ships. Land was used in common and buildings were built with local labor and resources. Humans continued to live for the most part within the ecological balance and in a system of sustainability, until the industrial revolution and the extraction of fossil fuels began.

The rest of this story about how we are now reaping the tragic consequences of out-of-control resource depletion and energy usage is well known. The work we do at the Shared Living Resource Center (SLRC) is in response to the wasteful, environmentally destructive, and socially intensive way we use land, build housing and other buildings, and transport ourselves. It has been our mission at SLRC to study, educate about, promote, design, and develop ways of creating stable, sustainable communities.

Continued "urban flight" will destroy our two greatest resources for ecologically sustainable living: the city and the Green Belt. There is also the broader regional and global ethical responsibility, based upon the Latin maxim *sic utere tuo ut alienum non laedas* (use your own property in such a manner as not to injure that of another).

We no longer have a choice; the time for denial is over. Ecologically sustainable community planning and design is in, and the old practice of using raw land for building energy-wasteful, detached houses as separate commodities is out.

The common characteristics of these new community forms are sharing of ownership, responsibilities, shopping, cooking and meals, child care, gardens, energy and resources, and cost savings in a residential cluster or village grouping.

We propose Shared Living Communities in context with a full array of companion social, economic, and environmental objectives. We are demonstrating how people can gain a sense of personal empowerment by sharing responsibilities with others on "common ground." We have placed ecological sustainability as the primary criteria and the highest priority in building community, for the poorest to the richest of people.

The work of rebuilding community is a complex and difficult challenge. But it can be very simple. Start with two, then three, then more people, share dinners, make agreements, do some projects, learn about each other's needs and values, and take down your backyard fences. Community begins with frequent face-to-face communication. It is that simple. Each community that organizes around the precepts discussed herein contributes directly to the ecological sustainability for all of us and the planet. You can really establish a self-reliant and ecologically sustainable rural community.

Considering the loose use of "green" terminology today, and how some designers, planners, and developers use socially and environmentally correct "design language" to describe their otherwise relatively conventional projects, we need to look more closely at what criteria should be present in an "ecologically sustainable community." We do not mean to dwell on semantics, but rather offer clarity to definitions that mean different things to different people.

"Ecology" refers to the system of interactions between organisms and their environment. An ecosystem contains energy, nutrients, and organisms within an environment functioning as one interdependent entity in context with human community, "ecological living" means a balanced interaction with the environment in ways that provide for the replenishment and healthy vitality of the larger whole.

This means more than just moving to the country and "living lightly on the land," but living fully with other people, working cooperatively, and sharing resources and responsibilities to create a lifestyle that is balanced and sustainable. However, writings by environmentalists and ecologists often fail to mention the ecological benefits of cooperating with others to share land, resources, and energy. People are part of an ecosystem as much as plants, animals, and soil are, so for an ecosystem to be healthy and vital, people must recognize how they play a powerful role in it. This means our lifestyles must take into account our interdependence with others and the land.

The word "sustainable" is often used in conjunction with terms such as agriculture, economy, culture, society, and family. It comes from the word "sustain," meaning to maintain and to supply with necessities. We call something sustainable when it provides for self-renewal and self-replenishing of a whole ecological system and maintains the continued vitality and health of that system. In our terms, this includes supporting and strengthening the human body and spirit to flourish and rejoice as an integral part of the ecosystem.

The term "community" derived its meaning from the common circumstances in which people effectively communicated on a daily basis in both a social and physical context. These person-to-person practices were the common social and civil experiences between groups of people in extended family, village, and larger community groups. In various village societies, people shared land in common, a practice that facilitated their survival through their ability to communicate.

The most meaningful communication often occurred in specially arranged places such as village squares, town halls, family dining and living rooms, churches, courtyards, plazas, "main streets," and even on trains. We identify community as a place for sharing responsibilities, economic and otherwise, for mutual benefit and survival, and as a place for social intercourse and shared activity marked by a feeling of unity and belonging, and expressed by individual participation. These are the conditions which foster communication that supports community.

With these definitions in mind, an "ecologically sustainable community" occurs only when all parts and processes of a system—

physical location, the natural environment, social and economic structure, physical and emotional health, spiritual, cultural, and personal
growth, and resource and energy use—are all sensitively integrated
and functioning with each other in a way that proceeds for the deep
harmony, well-being, and perpetuity of each part of the system and
the whole system. When this kind of harmonious process is working,
a more stable and cohesive community can take form, empowering
the larger group, and enabling personal empowerment to grow for
each member.

The "Eco" prefix, we feel, should only be used when certain
criteria are met, such as when car dependency is reduced by the self-
reliant/resource-sharing, extended-family, and village-cluster nature of
housing and intentional neighborhood designs that favor walking and
bicycling paths over car-dominated street systems.

Primarily, an Eco Village is low in energy and resource usage,
low in car-trip generation, and high in commonly owned properties
and amenities, high in democratic and participatory internal management, and high in voluntary and cooperative interaction between age,
income, cultural, and ethnic groups. In short, all of the criteria we
have presented for the Shared Living Community way of life.

The precursor models for Eco Villages have been well represented
with historic and now contemporary examples, such as existing Intentional Communities, the Urban Cooperative Block, and the numerous
cohousing communities being formed. An Eco Village is a transit node
made up of rich diversity of housing types and densities in a mixed-use,
composition approach, not just a conventional real estate development.

None of this discussion about Shared Living Communities, transit
systems, and Eco Cities as means to achieve ecological sustainability is
meaningful without addressing the Green Belt as an integrated policy
issue. The Green Belt is defined as a permanent physical, social, environmental, and economic process with its own self-contained rural
Eco Villages based upon sustainable agriculture and a stable, vital,
and cooperative rural society.

The locally revitalized rural economy is based upon direct
marketing of organic food to urban farmers' markets, food stores, and
restaurants, and a high level of self-sufficiency. Transit lines should
not be extended out to the rural Eco Villages unless there is a delib-
erate, regional planning strategy and enforceable policies to deter
development that attracts commuters from the city.

In the search for a harmonious and ecologically sustainable way of life, the asset we need to cultivate the most is the lost art of cooperation, or operating together for a common goal.

People today continue to seek a more secure place for their families to live within an imperfect world. It often takes a calamity to wake us up to the possible alternatives. The important thing is how we act in facing these challenges and whether we choose to enact positive new directions in our lives. The socioeconomic and environmental solutions to our present crises do not lie in each person's trying harder than before as lone individuals or isolated nuclear families, they lie in working more effectively with each other in a community system based upon cooperation.

The process of creating Shared Living Communities will involve making changes in land-use and development policies and the direct participation of people in creating their housing options. The precedents have been set by the success of International Communities and Cohousing in Europe and North America. The heritage goes deeper, however, with the success of the Kibbutzim in Israel, the cooperative housing movement throughout the world, and the present-day and historic example of the extended-family, village way of living.

To address this new movement will require major changes in strongly entrenched zoning ordinances, financing, and ownership methods, and a reeducation of both consumers and producers to become collaborators in the building of new extended-family communities in Eco Villages in both cities and the Green Belt.

At present, housing development in North America reflects the intertwined interests of lenders, developers, realtors, builders, and design professionals, with little or no involvement of the residents who will be the ultimate users. The key, therefore, lies in creating both a design form and a socioeconomic process that makes cooperating together a daily practice. It isn't what community costs but what it does for you, such as living more cheaply and saving time and having the social ambience of a small town.

The qualities that people are seeking in the small town way of life are community, less traffic, close proximity to local businesses and schools and services, knowing one's neighbors, and not having to commute. Can a small town be ecological, culturally interesting, socially diverse, and aesthetically pleasing? Can we move from the city seeking small town simplicity and not be bored to death? Is it possible to move to rural towns and not bring urban problems and growth with you? How can social interaction, participatory management, and ecological self-reliance of international communities be stimulated in a small town setting?

So, how do those who desire a small town atmosphere, complete with ecological design precepts, protection of open space and farmland, low dependence on automobiles, and extended family achieve it? In *Rebuilding Community in America* we presented the ecologically sustainable elements of the New Rural Town: "Imagine what a New Rural Town, rebuilt from a bypassed rural hamlet could be like.

"The town center contains mixed-use retail shops and offices, a medical clinic, a human and social services and cultural center, a library, schools, a telecommunication center, a meeting hall, restaurants, daily farm produce markets on the town plaza, live work spaces and community workshops, art and craft studios, a recycling center, and a transportation management center. Ecologically designed housing of varied types are clustered over the shops and around the town center."

The housing types could be community hotels for single people and travelers; a mixture of three-to-six bedroom, shared-living apartments; large, specially designed and clustered, six-to-ten-bedroom group houses; village clusters of twelve to twenty living units around a common house; and clustered, single-family houses interspersed throughout the community. Individual car trips would be limited because of the social and management agreements of the town to reduce the dependency on the car and because there is a car-sharing service. There would be high levels of food self-reliance through community gardens and well-equipped, local, food processing centers.

An intentional community approach could most effectively resuscitate a productive, small town quality of life in towns and villages that are stagnating, or dying out. In either case, the creation of a dynamic, interactive, self-reliant, and culturally creative, social, political, and economical structure will depend upon *a core group of residents* who can gain the support of others from within the town, or incoming new people attracted to the *community* objectives.

Challenges for the Future

by Lawrence R. Barker

The Napa Valley is not perfect. No place is. No community is. But the Napa Valley has been blessed in many ways which contribute to its identity as a community. Its basic geography—a valley between two lines of mountains with Mt. St. Helena to the north—gives it a clearly defined physical presence. It has a benign climate. Its fertile, volcanic soil is excellent for growing many crops. Its vineyards and wineries have established a vibrant industry based on fine wines and the "good life." Most importantly, it has a diverse population that cares deeply about the valley, and that is willing to devote time and resources to making the valley a better place.

Like all communities, the Napa Valley faces many challenges. Perhaps the greatest challenge is to perceive coming changes and take proactive measures to contain and ameliorate prospective problems. This is always difficult, as it is a natural human reaction to view the status quo as permanent. But all communities are continually in a constant state of change. The rate of change may vary. Some things may get better while others get worse. But there is no way to stop the clock, and there is no way to forestall change. In particular, the valley must deal with the pressures of growth: more people, more homes, more vineyards, more traffic. As the history of the valley demonstrates, these issues are best dealt with proactively.

Management of limited resources is always a challenge. In the late 1960s, a small group of forward-thinking Napans recognized that the growing population in the Bay Area, with its attendant suburban sprawl, represented a very real threat to a community based on agriculture. The office buildings and parking lots of Silicon Valley now cover some of the richest and most bountiful agricultural land in the entire nation. The Napa Valley responded by creating the Agricultural Preserve. Developed initially by the County Board of Supervisors and later confirmed by a vote of the population, the Agricultural Preserve places severe restrictions on the use and subdivision of land outside the cities. In short, the Agricultural Preserve restricts nonurban land use to residential and agricultural uses (including wineries). Subdividing property is prohibited unless the resulting parcels will each exceed 40 acres on the valley floor and 160 acres on the hillsides. The result is clear. With the Agricultural Preserve, the valley has maintained and fostered a community based on agriculture. Without it, the valley would be filled with shopping centers and housing subdivisions.

In the Napa Valley, water is in short supply. A growing population base, increased agriculture, and thirsty golf courses all consume increasing quantities of water. Most of the valley is dependent on well water, but the water tables throughout the valley are falling, and some are severely impaired. Wells have gone dry. In some cases, property owners have had to truck water into their properties—a cumbersome and expensive solution. The valley needs a comprehensive water management plan with certain areas requiring urban-style water systems to replace depleting wells.

This raises a second problem—the need for a governmental structure that can address the valley's needs. At present, the county's Board of Supervisors governs only the unincorporated areas, meaning that the cities in the valley make decisions that affect the valley well beyond their city limits. The Agricultural Preserve applies only in the county's unincorporated areas, but theoretically the cities could keep expanding their borders until they covered the whole of the county and the Agricultural Preserve disappeared. Since the incorporated and unincorporated areas are mutually dependent, it would make sense to have a single governing entity to resolve disputes between the cities and the unincorporated areas.

This leads to the issue of housing. With a population of approximately 125,000 (of which roughly half live in the City of Napa), the valley has a diffuse housing stock crossing a broad spectrum. However, the restrictions of the Agricultural Preserve, which strictly limits development, has put pressure on the cities in the valley to maintain a diverse housing stock in the face of rapidly rising real estate values. For the Napa Valley to continue to be a successful community, it must provide housing for all of the people who contribute to the life in the valley. That means housing for the workers in the wineries and the vineyards, for teachers and nurses, as well as for retired Silicon Valley millionaires, successful winemakers and vineyard owners.

The Napa Valley must also learn to manage tourism. For many years, the wineries have encouraged the flow of tourists, seeking to expose their wines to a larger and larger market. But tourists can be very hard on the places that they visit. They seek a kind of instant gratification which ignores the long-term ramifications. If the Napa Valley is going to continue to thrive, it must put the needs and concerns of its residents ahead of its tourists. Housing is more important than hotels. Traffic management must ensure that the valley is not so paved over for the tourists that it adversely affects both the quality of the life of the people who live in the valley as well as the microclimates that affect the quality of the vines.

The valley must not only continue to be a good place in which to live, but it must also offer economic opportunities to the people who live here. When the Agricultural Preserve was adopted in 1968, restrictions were put on subdividing property to make forty acres the minimum parcel size. At that time, it was perceived that forty acres was the minimum needed to support a family in viticulture. It was also acknowledged, with the then-prevailing land prices, that those people who dreamed of entering the wine industry could afford to do so, whether they were recent graduates of UC Davis or people seeking a midlife career change. Today, the rapid escalation of land prices coupled with the myriad restrictions on wineries have resulted in a situation in which only the very well-to-do can afford to come to the valley, buy land, and start a winery. There is a realistic fear that the children of the owners of today's wineries and vineyards will not be able to inherit them. Estate taxes and the rising need for capital will result in the wine industry being acquired piecemeal by large corporations and those who have made fortunes in places like Silicon Valley and Wall Street. Additionally, the valley has a shortage of opportunities for middle-management and executive positions. Other than the wine industry, restaurants, and retail stores restricted to the cities, there is little in the way of employment opportunities in the valley. For the valley to continue to be a place for those who live here and have come to love it, the valley must offer jobs for the children growing up here, with reasonable expectations for growth, advancement, and prosperity.

Finally, the valley must view its future in an inclusive, rather than isolationist, perspective. What happens in the neighboring areas will undoubtedly affect life in the valley. Indeed, the growth of population in the San Francisco Bay Area has a direct affect on life in the valley. We cannot preserve a way of life here without taking into consideration the life that goes on in adjacent areas.

The valley is truly a wonderful place to live. Whether it continues to be so will depend on whether it can successfully deal with the challenges of the future.

Tasting Wine

by Ruth Berggren

Robert Louis Stevenson wrote that Napa is "where the soil is sublimated under the sun and stars to something finer, and the wine is bottled poetry." It's true: creating great wine is an art, like painting or writing poetry. Although wines can be analyzed scientifically and precisely, great winemakers today rely on their own tastebuds more than on a scientific, test-tube approach. They trust their own senses. Like art, making wine and tasting wine are holistic, intuitive processes.

Like making art and wine, creating a community means combining different characteristics, colors, or flavors into a pleasing blend. The flavor combination of a community may be broken down "scientifically" into socioeconomic groups or statistics, but those analytical parts cannot be put back together to re-create the whole. Building community is also a holistic, intuitive process. In this book, we want to capture the essence of the Napa Valley community the way a wine taster captures the essence of a fine wine. The goal of this book is to allow the reader to drink in the culture, savor the community that has been cultivated here, and relish the way it has matured into The Good Life. We hope that you can experience the flavors and textures of the community by reading the tales in this book. We hope that you can distill essences from them that will linger on your palate.

Of course, the Napa Valley is a perfect place for this metaphor. It is a remarkably fruitful community, both literally and figuratively. Let's follow the metaphor of wine tasting, and see where it takes us. Tasting wine uses lots of senses. Taste is the most obvious sense used to judge wine, but it is not the only one. Of course, smell is very closely related to taste. But the color and clarity of wine—how it looks—is also important, as is its texture or "body"—how it feels. It is important to pay attention to all these sensual inputs while tasting wine. One should be open, attentive, and receptive as one enjoys wine. Each additional sense enhances the experience.

Taste

Taste, of course, is the primary element in wine tasting. Flavors found in wine are as diverse and unusual as peppermint, eucalyptus, coffee, earth, mold, oak, berries, pepper, yeast, petroleum, tobacco, wet dog, or steel. Our tastebuds are not deceiving us. Scientists can actually detect the esters associated with these flavors in wine. In fact, some 500 different chemical compounds are found in wine, some of them barely distinguishable. Some of the tastes are good; some are not. All of the tastes one experiences in a wine should be subtle and blended, so as not to overwhelm. The blending of these diverse flavors is the key to creating a fine wine.

In community, "good taste" is an important value. It is a truism (though often forgotten) that bigger is neither better nor more beautiful. One of the most obvious traits of the Napa Valley is that it has retained its small-town, rural feel, even in the face of the pressures of suburban sprawl. Merely 45 miles from San Francisco, it has struggled against being subsumed by the City. There has been a concerted and continuous effort since then to keep the small, rural community from becoming diluted by metropolitan sophistication and bigness. There have been heated debates about building a Saks Fifth Avenue, a Home Depot, and a bigger Safeway grocery store. Napans don't want Napa to look like every other place in the country. There are ongoing discussions about excessive tourism, too much traffic, and "houses on steroids." Even as it cultivates fine wine, fine food, and the Good Life, the community in the valley doesn't want to become too slick.

Good taste means, among other things, moderation, a balance between progress and tradition. In fact, good taste requires balance— a rich diversity of flavors or individuals blending with each other without clashing. In a fine wine, no single flavor overwhelms the palate. In a fine community, diverse groups work in harmony and balance with each other. In the Napa community, the owner of the winery and the worker in the vineyard are dependent on each other. They are equally important to the health of the community. That equivalence is an important social reality in the valley, and it is reflected in the significant role of women here. Anglo and Hispanic, men and women—they have to work together for this society to succeed. This requires balance. Everyone must be respected and nurtured to make a balanced community. As any child knows, if we lose our balance, we will fall.

Any community is made up of people with more differences than similarities. Just as the "wet dog" flavor in wine gives the wine complexity if it is subtle and ruins it if it is too noticeable, the balance of positive and negative flavors is critical. Too much sweetness is just as bad as too much "wet dog." What makes a community work—and what gives it character and weight—is the ability to emphasize the similarities while respecting and appreciating the differences. To ignore the differences is to lose sight of what makes a community strong. To focus on the differences is to destroy the sense of community. It is a balancing act and it requires constant vigilance.

Body

Wine has body. It has glycerin to give it body. A full-bodied wine will have "legs" running down the side of the glass when you tip it sideways. Wine is thicker than water. It holds together.

The "body" of the valley is its body politic. We talk about the Napa Valley as a community, but in reality it is several communities which, at different times, have widely divergent needs and goals. However, the Napa Valley has been able to meld those communities when the issues are momentous—for such difficult and potentially divisive issues as the Agricultural Preserve and the flood control measure for the Napa River.

A certain amount of stress is good for grapes. It is a maxim that low yield often results in higher quality wines. Similarly, in a community, bonds are stronger and more meaningful if they develop from conflict to consensus.

Complexity is a highly regarded trait in wine. It should not be "filtered out" or made homogeneous. It should be nurtured and encouraged. A community also draws strength from having people from different backgrounds, different races, and different cultures come together, offering different talents and abilities. Like many communities in this country, Napa struggles with the issue of diversity. The future depends on our ability to encourage complexity and to resist the homogenizing effect of gentrification.

Color

Color is important in telling the age of a wine. Young red wines are purple, especially around the edges. As they age, they take on a golden hue. A glass of red wine held to the light should be translucent, with a deep red center and a "halo" showing its age. The color of white wine also evolves—from a light yellow to a deep gold. Different varietals have different colors and intensities, so there are many "clues" to a wine's character in its color.

In Napa, the summer sky is bright blue, the grasses turn golden with the lack of rain, and the hills show off their oaks and evergreens, while oleander and wildflowers flourish in the abundance of sun. And, of course, the vineyards are green and lush, with the vines growing as much as an inch a day early in the season. When fall brings the rain, the hillsides burst with green and a whole new set of flowers bloom. Our first fall in the valley stunned us with its similarity to what we Midwesterners know as spring: brown turns to green; azaleas bloom; gardens are planted; and the rains renew the earth's fruitfulness. Only the vines themselves and some deciduous trees are in their skeletal winter browns. The sky may be cloudy, but most winter colors are vivid. Even the long evenings are enlivened by outdoor light displays that Napans use for two or three months to brighten the darkness. Spring is ushered in by the brilliant yellows of mustard and acacias. Fruit trees blossom, and the valley is awash in color. As the vineyards wake from their winter slumber, they change daily, growing more green and beautiful as they change from the brown of winter, through the yellows of spring, into the greens of summer.

This paean to the beauty of the valley may seem to have very little to do with "community," but there is an important connection. The people who live here enjoy these changes year after year. They watch them with deep joy and appreciation because they are acutely aware of how beautiful the valley is. Pleasure in the beauty of their surroundings is one of the special ingredients in this community. Most residents are grateful for the opportunity to live in this valley. And most people recognize that the privilege of living here carries with it a need for stewardship, an obligation to preserve and protect the natural beauty, and a responsibility never to take it for granted. So, the "color" of this community is not just its physical beauty, but also a conscious joy in and respect for that beauty.

Like wine, a community changes with time. The key is for it to *improve* with time.

Clarity
Clarity in wine means the wine is translucent. You can see through wine. Clarity proves a wine's purity. Nowadays, the science of winemaking has eliminated much of the problem with cloudy wines, and clarity is an absolute requirement in a fine wine. Otherwise, the wine will spoil.

Clarity in the valley is the clarity of the air when you can see from Mt. St. Helena north to Mt. Shasta in Oregon or west to the Farrallon Islands in the Pacific Ocean. It is also the clarity of vision of the leaders of the community. Vision and leadership are key qualities in a fine community. Otherwise, nothing gets done.

Finish
Finish is the lingering taste on your palate after you have swallowed wine. You have taken a sip, swirled it around on your tongue, sucked in some air through your mouth (to allow the aromas to reach your nose), and swallowed. The finish of a fine wine should be long and pleasant, not metallic or harsh.

A community should have staying power, the ability to stick with a problem until it arrives at a good solution. A community needs "fit and finish"—the ability to present a slick marketing image while preserving a down-home character for its locals. And a community should leave a good taste in our mouths when we leave it and head home to our own community, remembering experiences that nourish the mind, the body, and the soul.

How to use this book
We encourage you to use your senses to get to know the community presented in this volume. Listen to the stories. Taste the joy, and swirl it around on your tongue. Breathe in the perfume. Feel the passion for the land. Hold them up to the light and see the clarity of the visions that pull them together to work for the preservation of their community. And, after you have finished a chapter, notice how the story lingers on your palate and warms you. If you can experience the "bottled poetry" of the Napa community, we will have captured its essence more fully than any scientific analysis could do.

Summing Up

by Patton Howell

The Rollo May Connection

I think you might like to know the history of the Mind Age Series. On July 11, 1998, the fifth Rollo May Conversations began at the McComber home in Napa. It was about a new vision of community.

Rollo and I started these conversations twenty years ago. Now Rollo is dead, and his old friends have tried to carry on his thinking in these conversations. Rollo was a psychologist and best-selling writer. Each person was regarded by him with overwhelming wonder. Rollo was always looking for the cultural continuity of each person. He tried to find the right tone, rhythm, word, that this person could vibrate with. Community, he felt, was the key.

The first Conversation was in 1980. Four Nobel Laureates engaged in a discussion on the Convergence of Science and Religion. The ensuing book, *Nobel Prize Conversations*, is still selling and negotiations are underway for foreign publication. The second Conversation investigated the psychological basis of politics, and as a result the book *Politics and Innocence* was published and is also still selling today. The third Conversation resulted in a book, *Beyond Literacy*, a review of the deep cultural changes in modern reading. It won the Benjamin Franklin Award as the best book of nonfiction literature published in this country in 1990. Foreign language translations are underway. The fourth Conversation was held in Napa Valley at the home of the McCombers. This fourth conversation was published in full as the entire issue of the scientific journal, *Methods*. It revealed the startling cultural changes in store for us, and set the stage for this new book on how cultural changes can create a new vision for community.

Rollo called upon us all to "replace our existential despair with some myth of community. The culture of community is not something made by fate and foisted upon us. It takes community to create self and self to create community. Community is the ongoing flow of culture. There is no self except in interaction with community and no community that is not made of selves."

Once, in Amsterdam, Rollo was invited to meet with the Dalai Lama to discuss the cultural implications of the new surge of Buddhism in the United States. Rollo's position was: How can the highly organized intellectual structure of Buddhism fit into the much looser and more emotional structures of American Christianity?

The Dalai Lama said that there was little chance for an integration of dogma of the two religions—nor should there be. He predicted, however, that in terms of community the Buddhist and Christian cultures could integrate very successfully. It was only in community that the intimate interactions of people had the power to create a new vision of culture.

Mary Ann McComber's experiences bear this out. She is a Christian minister giving sermons at the Methodist Church in St. Helena, but is also a practicing Buddhist with close ties to the Dalai Lama's Buddhist community. However, within the new vision of community here in the Napa Valley she has found that the two religious cultures fit very well.

We decided that community should be the subject of the fifth Rollo May Conversations. You see the idea has been that these meetings should only be called in response to a timely and important cultural change.

Mary Ann over and over again has filled her house with experts from all over the world to participate in these Rollo May Conversations. In fact she contributed a highly regarded article in *Methods*.

It is important, I think, to mention the McComber home. Situated in the middle of Napa Valley, a volcanic hill rises out of a sea of vines. Their house is on the very top of the hill. The tree-lined drive is a mile long, finally winding up the hill. Their home is a haven of peace in this harried world. The view is of mountains and sky with the Napa Valley laid out below. It is the perfect place for discussions on the future of the world. Since we are all "spousal" here, her husband Don McComber, a retired insurance executive, and my wife Joan have participated fully in the community move to get this fifth book finished and to you.

I'd like to tell you a story about Rollo's final connection to this land. Rollo was dying at his home in Tiburon, an hour's drive from Napa. One day Rollo whispered, "Tell my brother, Pat Howell, that I'm dying." The same day Mary Ann went down to her beloved old Indian burial grounds. To get there from her house she crosses the vine-filled land to the trees running into the Napa River. Under the trees, she saw the obsidian glint of an arrowhead among the fallen leaves and stooped down to pick it up. There were an unusual number of hawks circling over her and one dive-bombed as she had her hand on the arrowhead. She looked up . . . and saw Rollo, the wind blowing his long hair. He was so tall and beautifully handsome. He was standing on the bank of a river. He waved to her and turned to cross the river, "No," she called, "don't go; you can't come back." But Rollo had crossed over and was climbing up a mountain on the other side. He turned back to look at her and seemed to say, "Oh, I will come back in many ways."

Then Mary Ann was back among the trees with her hand on the arrowhead. She looked at her watch. It said five o'clock. Rollo died at five o'clock on that day. I like to think that this book is one of the ways his spirit has come back.

Community

Community is where we receive culture and how we create culture. Rational theories of community are abstractions. They are snapshots of an unending cultural flow. Culture must be lived as art if we are to understand it. Cultural art is how culture is passed on through the millenniums. One of the great examples of art is "Liberty Leading the People" by Delacroix. It is of the French Revolution. However, in showing a bare-bosomed young lady holding the flag aloft, the scene speaks of freedom without abstracting it. In fact it gives no rational information about where it is or how things turn out. Nevertheless, it is an enduring metaphor of community for the French.

Art is not just painting. There are vast constructions of past communal living in Machu Picchu in Peru, and in Angkor Vat in Cambodia. You have read of the revival of Spanish Opera in the valley—the Zarzuela—by William Jarvis, of plays and play writing at the White Barn by Nancy Garden, and musical concerts ringing out all through the community; even business becomes an art form here. Writing of all kinds flows forth in this community.

Ruth Berggren and Mary Ann McComber have engaged all the arts of the valley to bring you this book. They have devoted a year and a half to the task of interviewing the inhabitants, asking them in many ways, "Why are we so comfortable here? How did it all happen? What is the secret of Napa Valley?" The results of these recorded interviews have been meticulously edited by Ruth Berggren.

These are real living people embarked on a new vision of community. These new visions found in Napa Valley are not abstract rules, but rather art which will apply to anyone in any community. For example, there is a sense of self-confidence among the people of this valley. There is the remarkable ability of the community to use government rather than allowing the government to use the community— Power to the People. State Senator John Vasconcellos, who was at the Rollo May Conversations on community, said, "Government is what happens to people when they can't work together."

In terms of the Napa River, the people told the United States government what to do, and the Army Corps of Engineers wrote, "The success of this collaboration serves as a model—not just for Napa, but for the nation." Paul Battisti, a leader of the Napa Community Coalition for a Flood Management Plan added, "In the years to come history will judge the fact that citizen participation must take place *during* the planning process."

A planned community was organized by the Disney Company in Florida in 1995. Its name was Celebration. Its goal was to be a place where neighbors greeted neighbors and children chased fireflies, where the movie house showed cartoons on Saturday.

Unfortunately citizen participation didn't take place "during the planning process" in Celebration. World-famous architect Philip Johnson designed the public buildings, and to keep everything perfect, the people who live in Celebration are restricted to the ratio of grass to shrubs to trees on their lots and to white curtains in their windows. The streets are swept each night.

The Disney Company confused the appearance of a community with the cultural spirit of a community. Celebration is an abstraction of community. Nothing happens except a civil, safe existence. Celebration is a dead community, as well maintained as a cemetery.

We know who we are in the valley. As Brian Kelly says, "It is geopolitical. The political and geographic boundaries are the same. We're surrounded essentially by mountains." If you don't have mountains, how about a river or a shore, or a spirit as a boundary?

Self-confidence means feeling good about where you are. That is not a rational idea of a way to live, but it is the reality of the way people do live in the valley. Five million tourists come each year. Many of them come to be married. It isn't that they want to live here. It's for luck. This is a lucky place. Self-confidence creates luck. You can take the luck with you as you leave.

Another facet of this new vision of community is the way diverse people live together. Immigrants to the valley were first Spanish and Russians. Citizens of the United States arrived in the 1850s—Germans, Irish, Scots, English, and Africans. Following these settlers came the Chinese. The valley became a mixture of ten ethnic groups.

How come they get along together so effectively? One thing, people who live in the valley are here because they want to be here. They weren't sent. They came. Another thing, "diverse individuals" describes people here rather than groups of race, sex, or class. Power to diverse, unique individuals tends to drive out competing ethnic power centers of diverse groups. Individual diversity means that there are more differences within groups than there are differences between groups—for example, in the valley you can't tell whether a person is rich or poor by differences in clothing or hair styles. There is little difference among ethnic groups as to basic modes of transportation, education, percent going to college. There are few housing tracts here. Big homes and little homes are mixed in together. There is no "other side of the railroad tracks" to live on here. There are "poor" people here, but no "poor" neighborhoods.

I'm using the term, diverse individuals. Ron Birtcher calls such people collective individuals. People here are more than group identity, and also more than rules about the social identity one should have. In fact "identity" doesn't cut it here. We find self-knowledge and self-confidence in the living interactions within our community. It's like being fully alive. Being fully alive can also be your way. And you can take it back home when you leave Napa Valley.

Brian Kelly uses the word *spousal*. "Events are spousal—you are expected to bring your spouse with you. Where do children fit into this? It's not just that my wife goes with me, so do my children. Our kids always went with us."

This kind of community becomes a balance—a rich diversity of individuals, displacing, combining with, and representing each other. Individual value, power, and meaning find equal weight. They are in harmony and balance with each other. "Equivalent" is from the latin *aequus* (equal) combined with *valens* (to be worth). Equivalent is an appropriate word to stand for diversity in balance. No one person overwhelms the others. The worker in the field and the owner of a vineyard become equivalent. There is the balance of many equivalent individuals becoming greater than the sum of the parts. Equivalency is how these diverse people of Napa function so efficiently. Equivalency can work in your own community.

Robert Louis Stevenson wrote that the Napa Valley is "where the soil is sublimated under the sun and stars to something finer, and the wine is bottled poetry." Great wines and great food are the material products of the Napa Valley. But what is more important is a new vision of community which makes the material things happen. This vision is based on paying attention to culture.

Think of the community culture within which your thinking has grown, as a kind of water. Now think of a fish swimming in the water. The fish is unaware of the water. But when the fish is out of the water, the fish is very aware of its absence. Cultures are like water. Waves of thought come through that water. The meanings of conversations are often received as waves of sound, sight, and thought. Our psyches are bombarded daily with the art of thought. This is our culture.

In the evolution of community, human interactions that are most successful tend to survive. What is successful evolves and is passed on in rhythms of individual lives interacting with the dynamic life of community—a cultural continuum extending back to the archaic past. People in the valley tend to live with their selves in balance with a cultural feedback loop. Culture to self and self to culture—both grow. This is not an abstract identity but a true, living, growing self.

This is why the people in the Napa Valley think differently. It is the hardly noticed waves of thought vibrating through the day that are the basis of a new vision of community. People tend to see things culturally—not in the abstract—more like the reality of art.

Here is an example, all of us have been taught that we have free will. In other words, when we choose to do something we actually do it. But when we check this out in our own lives, we find that we rarely actually do what we had rationally chosen. If we think about this, we may become aware of an unnoticed will in our lives lying behind our abstract will. It seems to be a collective kind of cultural will. It is like waves of thinking filling our days. But in the pace of urban life people have forgotten how to notice this thinking. People in the valley do notice this cultural thinking. It is a way of thinking based on the way people interact here. A cultural will, on the whole, decides what they will do. They pay attention to the waves of cultural thought in daily living—the rhythms, music, grace, patterns, stray words that fill up their lives.

This kind of thinking is like tuning a piano. Electronic meters can be precise about sound as abstraction, but they can't be precise about the overall quality of sound. Only a human being can be precise about that. It is a cultural way of thinking. It is an art that is used in the valley in every aspect of people's lives. Unique cultural perception of diverse individuals nevertheless come to communal conclusions.

People in the valley are fond of saying, "What I did seemed crazy, but you see it turned out to be right." "Crazy" here often means cultural choices for what one actually does rather than abstract, "free will" choices.

In this new vision of community that is growing in Napa Valley, it becomes essential for businesses to learn the new cultural language of the valley. Brian Kelly writes about businesses that are already oriented that way. Dana Leavitt and Don McComber bring up MBWA, which means "management by walking around," a way of being open to the cultural environment. One listens for the waves of thought, the rhythms, patterns, words, that are hardly noticed. This practice can spread beyond the valley. You can take it with you.

Don McComber tells how large corporations can use and be used by this new community vision. Think of a community where private people make the choices that govern their lives. Part of that is choosing businesses that can pay attention to community. One of the biggest business challenges in the valley is the creation of affordable housing for the inhabitants. The challenge is to keep rich and poor living together, as is now the case in the valley. Ken Norwood proposes a structure for eight families in a cluster that takes a minimum lot size and can be mixed into more affluent neighborhoods and even into downtown.

As Jeff Redding says, "In the valley people think of education as cultural art." It is important to teach cultural thinking. The story of McCormick Ranch is an example of that thinking. And if you will notice, the stories in this book are all examples of the art of passing on community. Communicating through cultural art is the language of the valley.

People who feel good about the community need a language that is real, that deals with cultural thoughts. Abstract rational thinking is a useful tool in this new vision, but the people need something more basic, such as cultural thinking. The most important element of being comfortable in a community is knowing that cultural life is being passed on in the little, unnoticed, everyday living of the inhabitants. It becomes an everlasting tradition.

The kind of cultural thinking practiced in these stories of the valley can be taken along with you to any place in the world. And they work, not as rules but as cultural art. It has been a pleasure to those putting this book together. We have told you some of our stories. Community is the process of telling each other stories. We need to tell each other our stories. We would like you to share your stories with us. Write us. Communities are always growing. We need to grow together.

Mary Ann McComber has a final story to tell about telling stories.

When Ruth Berggren and I began interviewing people in the valley, week after week people shared with us their stories. We discovered that we were a part of their stories, never having understood that before. Week after week each person interviewed gave back memories of who we were. Slowly over the months the stories continued, and we began feeling differently, more calm, more whole, more trusting, and certainly more understanding of who all these friends are, and of who we are. This was the beginning of a whole new dimension of love and compassion. These are the gifts that were bestowed upon us in this place we call home.